Designing Orientation

Chris van Uffelen

Designing Orientation

signage concepts & wayfinding systems

BRAUN

contents

PREFACE 6

RELAXED WAYFINDING
LIVING, CULTURE, LEISURE, SHOPPING

Alexander Owen Architecture Resorts World Birmingham Wayfinding and Placemaking System 10

Moscow Design Studio / Polina Chemeris Museum of Russian Impressionism 14

Entro Friday Harbour 18

studio polylog Wayfinding Zeche Zollverein 22

Endpoint Dubai Design District (d3) 26

TERADADESIGN ARCHITECTS Toshima Ecomusee Town 30

Wayfinding Consultores OPK Kennedy 32

Moniteurs Communication Design Kunsthalle Mannheim 36

Kolektyf Residential Property in Krakow 40

polyform – planen und gestalten Museumsinsel Berlin James-Simon-Galerie 44

Sägenvier DesignKommunikation Inselhalle Lindau 48

Benedek & Co. Brand & Design Soulmade Wayfinding System 52

Endpoint / Pentagram Design Harrods – Wayfinding Strategy 54

Sunder-Plassmann & Werner Highlighting the Elegance of the Alte Pinakothek 58

INTELLIGENT WAYFINDING
LEARNING, STUDYING, RESEARCHING

SKOLNICK Architecture + Design Partnership Jackie & Harold Spielman Children's Library 64

inkl. Design Inclusion Guidance System 68

Studio Semaphore Deakin Downtown 72

Studiostaak Amsterdam Public Library 76

22quadrat FHZ Orientation System 80

P-06 Atelier St Dominic's International School 84

Kuhl|Frenzel Guidance and Orientation System for the FernUniversität in Hagen 86

Form & Fokus Deutsches Biomasseforschungszentrum, DFBZ 90

Wayfinding Consultores PUC Center for Innovation 94

Studio Eva Plass with Benedikt Haid Philologicum – Subject Library LMU Munich 98

BUSINESS WAYFINDING
WORKING, FILING, MEETING

Renda Helin Design & Interiors Emre Group Head Office 104

SLANG – Studio for graphic design Google and YouTube Offices in Berlin 108

La Letterie Châteauform' City Paris Les Puces 112

büro uebele visuelle kommunikation HypoVereinsbank Building Wayfinding System 114

designgruppe koop Barrier-Free Orientation and Signage System Landratsamt Ostallgäu 118

6D-K Azusa Sekkei Office Sign 122

studio kw. kommunikationsdesign Guidance System SOKA-Dach 124

Alexander Owen Architecture Peckham Levels Wayfinding System 128

buero bauer Gesellschaft für Orientierung und Identität aws Headquarters Signage 132

Moniteurs Communication Design Merck – Innovation Center 134

Form & Fokus Dresden Chamber of Trades and Crafts 138

IFUB* GfK Berlin 142

Studio SÜD-Visuelle Kommunikation Edelrid-Signaletik 146

Blitz SAGE Publications 150

unit-design ECB – Signage and Information System 152

C&G Partners Hearst Tower 156

Crossboundaries, Beijing Aimer Lingerie Factory Complex 158

büro uebele visuelle kommunikation Stuttgart Region Chamber of Commerce and Industry, Signage System 162

Kolektyf Nowy Targ 166

FAST WAYFINDING
HEALING, TRAVELING, PARKING

ArtHouse Design Children's Hospital Colorado 172

Pentagram Parking at 13-17 East 54th Street 176

6D-K Kawagoe – Blood Donation Room 178

P-06 Atelier Lisbon Cruise Terminal 180

buero bauer Gesellschaft für Orientierung und Identität Caritas Daycare Center 182

TERADADESIGN ARCHITECTS Minami Oral Health Clinic 184

Dotdash Queensland Children's Hospital 186

DESIGNERS INDEX 190

PICTURE CREDITS 191

City of Westminster.
1911
TO HOUNSLOW
9 MILES
TO LONDON
[HYDE PARK CORNER]
1 MILE

preface

chris van uffelen

Complex systems require clear rules: Somewhere between a single-family home and an international airport signage systems and wayfinding design become inevitable. In the private home, a "May I use your toilet?" is quite normal but missing or wrong signage to the restrooms at JFK International Airport not only costs nerves, but also leads to enormous superfluous streams of people, to countless unnecessary and often unsatisfactory attempts of conversation and possibly even to worse... Because of this, every architect will have to deal with the issue of designing orientation sooner or later, if he doesn't want anyone to put up any kind of signs. Basically, he or she is already involved in the design, but making it obvious is often a second step.

This is the subject of this book. It shows how architecture and signage can harmonize with each other, how they can support each other, how one benefits from the other. Sometimes architecture is in the foreground and the wayfinding system is discreetly withdrawn, sometimes the signage attracts all eyes, deliberately setting aesthetic accents in the spatial structure. Often – and ideally – architects or interior designers plan hand in hand with graphic designers and signage experts from the very beginning. Especially when a CI has to be taken into account and integrated in the signage. In such cases, entire graphic systems have to come together with the buildings. But even with new, independent signage systems that do not have to care about a building or a CI an inherent logic must be developed at the beginning alongside a graphic idea. What is needed to find orientation in the entire space and its parts? Basically it is the same problem that the editor of the "Almanac de Paris" faced in 1779 when he wanted to describe the buildings of the city: Marin Kreenfelt de Storcks first used the numbering of the street lamps to identify the individual houses, but then assigned numbers to each front door independently – the birth of the house number, an extremely simple but very efficient orientation system. Since then, countless systems have been developed, but only a few of them have had a comparable influence. The best known is probably the pictogram and color scheme that Otl Aicher developed from 1967 to 1972 as the design commissioner for the Olympic Games in Munich. At that time the general, international comprehensibility of such signs became more and more important and accordingly efforts began to unify important systems: In 1968 the Vienna Convention on Road Signs and Signals was adopted, and in 1971 the additional agreement to the Convention on Road Signs and Signals was adopted, which unified the latter – across the Iron Curtain – in most European countries as well as in South American and Asian countries. Colors, shapes, lettering, numbers, pictograms and arrows – these are the components of both traffic signs and wayfinding systems presented here. But the individual wayfinding systems do often add a haptic orientation as well: Models and Braille are important elements which enable blind people to orientate themselves in space. But also in the choice of materials the systems presented here go far beyond the usual traffic signage: wood, bronze, vinyl, acrylic, individually painted signs show that these examples are not only about orientation but that the assumed applied graphic of signs is rather a kind of art that stages the client – be it a cultural institution or a company, a hospital or a department store – thus contributing to its image and also adding value to the architecture.

← ↙ ↓ Different signage systems in London

living

culture

shopping

relaxed wayfinding

leisure

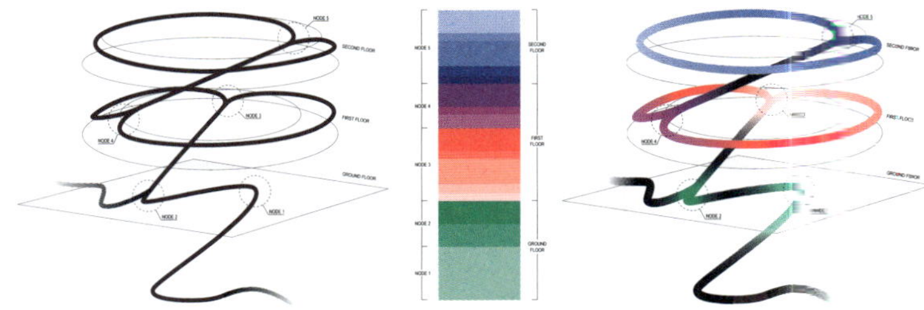

Resorts World Birmingham Wayfinding and Placemaking System

↖ View from the ground floor up to first floor
↑ Escalators

↑↑ Color analysis diagram
→ View from lower ground floor entrance

Designer Alexander Owen Architecture
Location Birmingham, United Kingdom
Client Genting
Completion 2020
Paint contractor Bagnall's
Vinyl contractor Bowden & Dolphin
Function Retail

For this, the first in a series of placemaking installations building upon their new color-coded wayfinding system, Alexander Owen focused on the key space for guests, the central three-story atrium. His response to the brief was an architecturally-responsive visual art piece that celebrates the structure, form and organization of the building, as well as importantly the flow of visitors within it. The graphic form of the artwork as well as the relationship between the various colors have been driven by a three-dimensional analysis of the space. In this sense it's not simply art applied to the surface of the architecture, it's art entirely driven by the architecture itself. The colors themselves have been selected to work both independently and as a family to engender different moods and feelings.
The purples and pinks inspire and provide a vibrant energy, whilst the blues and greens exude more healing, tranquil energies. Black has been used to fill the neutral voids between the floors and act as a backdrop to the color. Whilst pink and yellow fluorescent stripes have been incorporated at UK average male and female eye-heights to reveal a sense of human scale within the atrium and tell the story of how guest's flow through the space. Together, the movement within the graphic form and the energy of the changing chromatic hues are intended to increase dwell time, draw guests through the space and encourage exploration of what Resorts World has to offer.

cineworld
GBK
Burger
BUNCH
LOWER GROUND
5 SKY BY THE WATER
VIA HOTEL LOBBY LIFTS
2 VOX CONFERENCE CENTRE
SPA
-1 RESTAURANTS

↑ View from ground floor node 2

↓ View up to first floor node 3 and second floor node 5

↗ View up to first floor node 4

→ Detail showing fluorescent stripe

→→ View up to first floor node 3

CASINO &

МАГАЗИН
SHOP
БОЛЬШОЙ ЗАЛ
GRAND HALL

Museum of Russian Impressionism

Designer Moscow Design Studio / Polina Chemeris
Location Moscow, Russia
Completion 2016
Architect John McAslan + Partners
Typeface Brutal
Function Public

The museum is housed in the building which earlier, at the end of the 19th century, has been used as a mill by Bolshevik factory. This building is remarkable for its unusual shape – it is a cylinder with a rectangular parallel piped on the roof. The mill was successfully restored and converted into a modern museum by the British architectural bureau John McAslan + Partners, which was opened to the public in 2016. The interior of the museum is extremely minimalistic. The main light gray color of the interior does not distract visitors from the art. The signage is integrated very subtly to keep the minimalistic approach, most of the signs are painted directly onto the walls. Visually the system is based on the logo and a graphic motif from the metal cladding of the façade. Stripes with tapered ends form plenty of distinct pictograms and numerals shaping an own graphic language.

← Directional signage to shop and grand hall

↑ Pictograms

↓ Directional signage with pictogram, lift

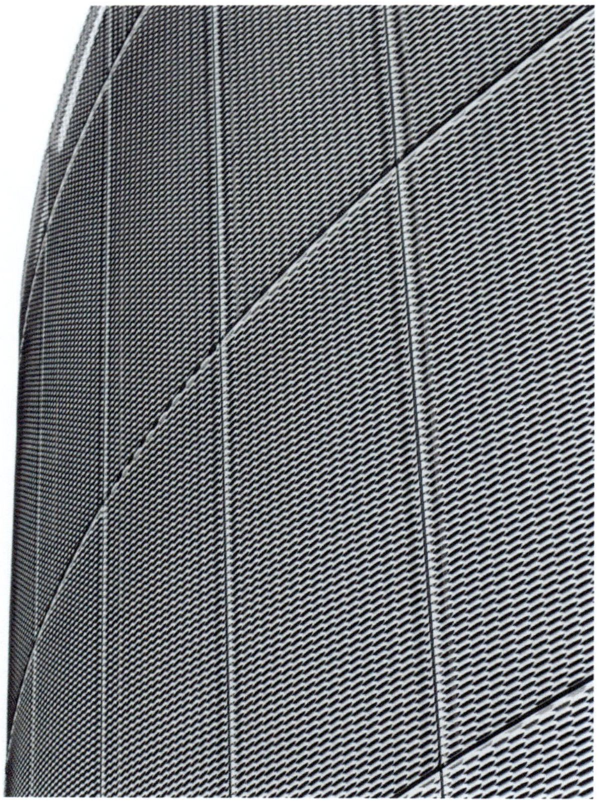

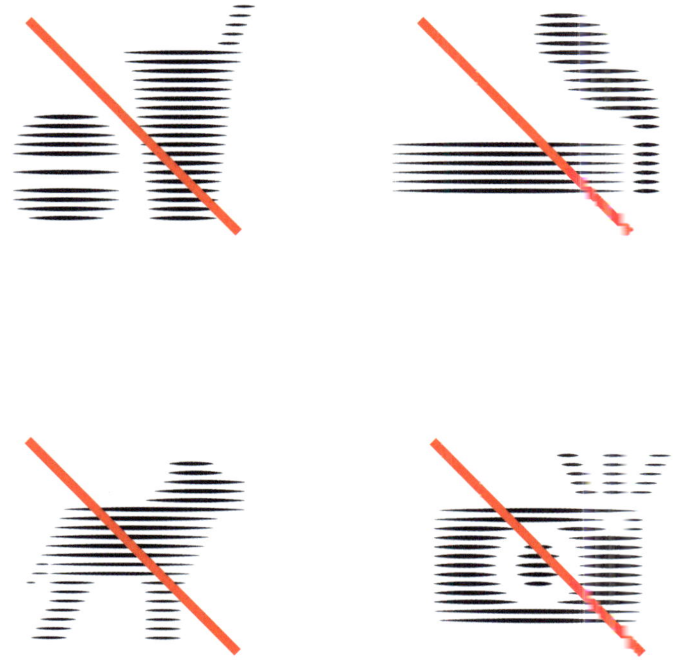

↑ Façade, metal cladding
↓ Directional signage, painted onto the wall

↑ Prohibition signs
↓ Directional signage, wardrobe

→ Directional signage, exit

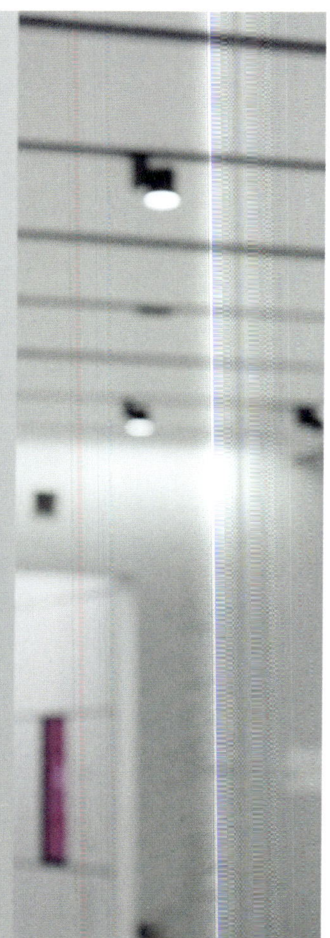

ВЫХОД
EXIT
КАССЫ
TICKET OFFICE
ГАРДЕРОБ
WARDROBE
ИНСТАЛЛЯЦИЯ «ДЫШАЩЕЕ ПОЛОТНО»
INSTALLATION "BREATHING CANVAS"

SPRUCE LOOP
SUGAR MAPLE WAY

Friday Harbour

<u>Designer</u> Entro
<u>Location</u> Innisfil, Ontario, Canada
<u>Client</u> Friday Harbour
<u>Completion</u> 2019
<u>Typeface</u> Avenir
<u>Function</u> Living and recreation

Friday Harbour, on the shores of Lake Simcoe, was designed to be a destination where every day feels like a Friday, all year-round. It involves the excavation of the existing marina basin and the construction of the largest in-land marina in Canada. The 600-acre development (2.42 square kilometers) includes an entire community with luxury town homes and condos, recreational amenities, a nature trail system, a network of streets that serve pedestrians, vehicles, and a system of shuttles, as well as an extensive retail area. As part of the resort development, an extensive and unique signage program was a must.
Entro designed the exterior signage program with the intention of creating a sense of unity among the resort's different environments and offerings. A sophisticated, minimal font and color palette communicate the quality and tranquil beauty of the resort and worked with the overall brand position the

↖ Exterior pylon
↓ Bird's-eye view

↑ Golf course pylon
← Golf course pylon

resort had developed. Within the seven kilometers of trails, interpretive signage tells the story of the site's history, as well as conservation efforts underway.

A particular focus of the work was on signage for The Nest, the resort's award-winning 18-hole golf course, designed by world-renown course designer, Doug Carrick. Working closely with the resort and golf club staff, Entro created a signage program that is very much a departure from an off-the-shelf collection of signs common to most golf courses, and instead, extended the style of the resort's signage to the greens. Golfers have remarked on the unique sense of place and the distinct, "reinvented" experience evoked by the signage.

↑ Washroom signage
↓ Exterior pylons

↑ Washroom signage
↓ Exterior map

↗ Exterior identification signage
→ Retail signage

BEACH CLUB

CHECKOUT
FH Fine Food

MUSEUM

Wayfinding Zeche Zollverein

Designer studio polylog
Location Essen, Germany
Client Landesentwicklungsgesellschaft NRW
Completion 2010
Architect OMA/AMO
Landscape designer Agence Ter
Typeface DIN
Function Culture

In 2001, the industrial complex Zeche Zollverein in Essen was declared a World Heritage Site by UNESCO. This is a high distinction that calls for the preservation of the colliery buildings as a monument and the communication of their significance, but also for an innovative concept for revitalizing and making the site usable for the public. The wide range of activities on offer at Zollverein with permanent and temporary exhibitions, major events, conferences and meetings, the spaciousness of the site and the diversity of visitors place high demands on the orientation system.
The challenge was above all to meet the demands of over 500,000 visitors per year while taking into account the strict requirements of the preservation of historical monuments.

↑ 3D model in the terrain to give an overview of the large area

← Illuminated lettering with escalator
↓ Plans to go with current information

Every person orientates himself differently, sets different visual priorities. Individual solutions with flexible usage options are in demand. The scenic contours and the outstanding buildings are important clues for determining the location and destination. The intention of the designers, formerly known as f1rstdesign, was to create an orientation system without conventional signs. After the site had been cleared of old pollution and preserved, a clear route had to be created that was visually restrained and avoided a forest of signs. To ensure a better overview for the international guests, the buildings at Zollverein were numbered consecutively – like houses in a city. This system is familiar to everyone and nobody has to be able to read and understand complicated building names. Models of the grounds – adequately in rusty steel and cast bronze – serve as a general overview and as tactile access for the visually impaired. Hand plans are constantly updated.

↑ World of orientation
↗ Pictograms
← House number, each building is numbered
↓ 3D model for hand scanning and with Braille

↗ Ground guides
↗↗ Raised letters of ground guides
→ Illuminated lettering, made of special effect Plexiglas

HALLE 5

ممنوع التدخين
NO SMOKING
TARSILA
SCHUBERT

Dubai Design District (d3)

Designer Endpoint
Location Dubai, United Arab Emirates
Client TECOM Group
Completion 2018
Typeface English: DIN / Arabic: DIN Next LT Arabic
Function Culture & public

Dubai Design District, known as d3, is home to the creative thinkers in the region, an event hub and a tourist magnet. With an open courtyard footprint, ever-increasing footfall, an evolving retail, food and beverage and office landscape, managing the crowd as well as every day commuters can be a challenge. Events are always happening and the need for accurate, flexible and up-to-date information is key to make the overall user experience enjoyable. Endpoint developed a masterplan wayfinding strategy that focuses on the entire user journey. Introducing a zoning system was a central part of the strategy with such a large and expanding site. Color coding connects the above and below ground levels. Supersized freestanding numbers were introduced to highlight the easily missed building entrances. At the same time, Endpoint's wayfinding design reflects the d3 brand, which creates a sense of place. On top of that, placemaking site markers became landmarks helping visitors create a mental map of the district, whilst adding interest and photographic opportunities.

↖ Entrance area for Design Quarter
← Building identification number
↓ Fire equipment pictogram

↑ Pick up and drop-off area
↓ Directional signs

↑ Pedestrian orientation for Design Quarter
↓ Basement wall graphics

↗ Supersized freestanding numbers
→ Basement lift lobby graphics

Letterheads
Photocopying
Scanning
Binding Services

مستوى
Level
B1

Toshima Ecomusee Town

↖↖ Signs in the exterior area
↖ Signs in the entrance area
↓ Signpost concept
↑ Floor plates with signposts
→ Signs in front of the elevator

<u>Designer</u> TERADADESIGN ARCHITECTS
<u>Location</u> Tokyo, Japan
<u>Completion</u> 2015
<u>Function</u> Mixed use

TERADADESIGN ARCHITECTS handled the signage and graphic design for the common-use areas of the composite facility "Toshima Ecomusee Town", which is comprised of a ward office, shops, and apartment dwellings. The architects' signage plan incorporated the usage of a variety of sign panels that measured in the same 1:6 vertical/horizontal proportions as the Eco veil panels. These signs would heighten the sense of integration between the architecture and its interiors, and by using different materials for the panels depending on their usage and location – wood grain for the ward office, glass for the shops, stainless steel for the common-use areas, and black stainless steel for the apartment complex – the architects have conceived a signage system that would guide people on an intuitive level through this composite facility.

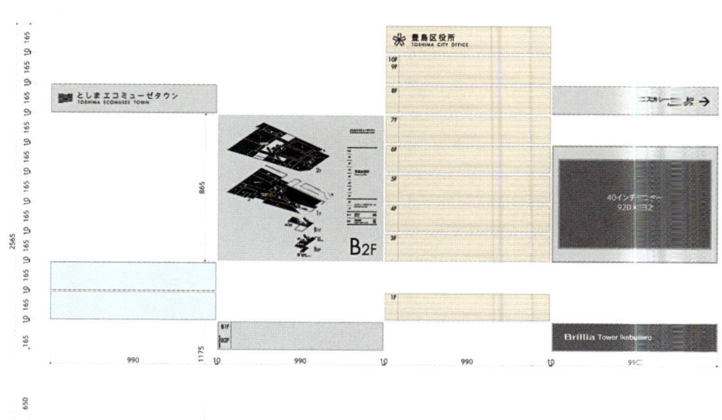

としまエコミューゼタウン

4
ACCESO
MALL
HOMY · TOTTUS
SODIMAC

Ascensor
ACCESO MALL
2½
3
HOMY
RED
HÚMEDA
2½

OPK Kennedy

Designer Wayfinding Consultores
Location Santiago, Chile
Client Falabella SA
Completion 2019
Architect Eduardo Silva Architects
Typeface Lato
Function Retail

The Open Plaza Kennedy (OPK) shopping center is a large commercial development (140,000 square meter) located east of Santiago. It is composed of five storys dedicated to shops which had to be connected to ten existing parking floors. The OPK posed an interesting wayfinding dilemma for customers, some of whom had to park on in-between floors. Wayfinding Consultores sorted out this problem by naming middle-ground floors "y medio floor" (half floor in Spanish), a colloquial expression that permitted the shopping center to establish a relaxed conversation with its users. To facilitate people's orientation, each floor was painted with a color palette that relates to the different regions and landscapes of Chile, creating a meaningful and pleasant experience for customers.

← Large-scale signage in parking
↙ Large-scale signage

↑ Indoor directional sign
↓ Pictograms

↑ Indoor directional sign
↓ Large-scale signage

→ Large-scale signage

3
ACCESO
MALL
HOMY · TOTTUS
SODIMAC HOMECENTER

DERKREIS FÜR DIE KUNSTHALLE MANNHEIM E.V.
ÜLLER
FUCHS PETROLUB SE
LER-STIFTUNG
BRIGITTE & JÜRGEN STRUBE
HEINRICH-VETTER-STIFTUNG
ANNHEIMER VERSICHERUNG AG
FAMILIE GROTHE
B. METZLER SEEL. SOHN & CO. KGAA
SAP SE
BASF SE
DR. CARL FRIEDRICH REISS
LANDESBANK BADEN-WÜRTTEMBERG
FIRMA SAX & KLEE
HANS UND INGE BICHELMEIER
H.W. & J. HECTOR
INFO
GUIDES
TICKETS

Kunsthalle Mannheim

Designer Moniteurs Communication Design
Location Mannheim, Germany
Client Stiftung Kunsthalle Mannheim
Completion 2018
Architect gmp - Architekten von Gerkan, Marg und Partner
Interior designer OH-Studio
Typeface Akkurat Mono
Function Culture

In analogy to the space-creating elements of the city – house and block, street and square – the Kunsthalle Mannheim offers visitors varied tours through closed and open spaces with changing insights and views. The analogue and digital visitor guidance system blends in with the architecture in terms of design, thereby significantly supporting the identity of the building. The decisive design features were developed on the basis of the architecture, large but not too large, easy to read, directly on the wall rather than on a support, framed – pure, clear, direct. The architectural grid is adapted to a unit of measurement suitable for the guidance system and serves as the basis for arrangement and order. This imaginary grid gives the information its graphic support. It can also be found on the façade in the transparent metal mesh.

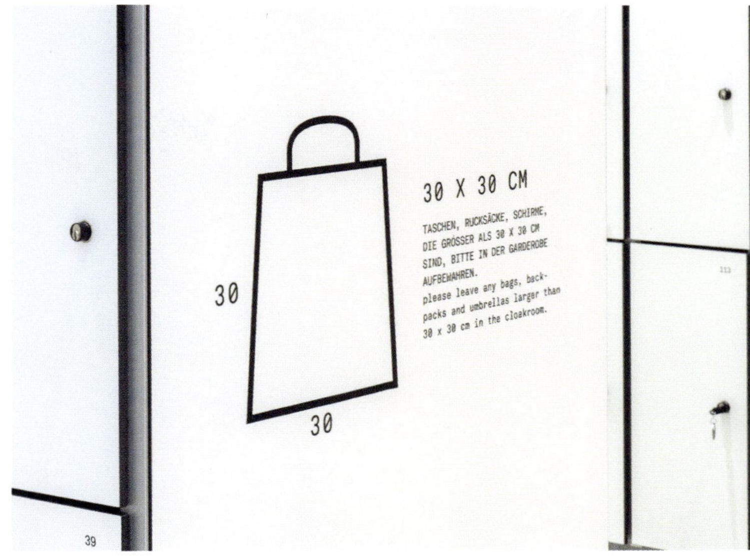

← Foyer
↓ Kunsthalle Mannheim exterior view

↑↑ Pictogram on lockers
↑ Pictograms

↑ Direction and destination marking applied directly to the wall with paint
↓ Digital and analogue signage

↓ Signage on the wall, toilets

↗ Illuminated cube at the counter
→ Exhibit with description on the wall

CKETS
JEFF WALL. APPEARANCE
2. Juni bis 9. September 2018
INFO
INFO
DIE AUSSTELLUNG
the exhibition

KUBUS 6
ANSELM KIEFER
ZWISCHEN FORM UND ANTI-FORM
between form and anti-form

WYJAZD

winda
lift
schody
stairs
H

Residential Property in Krakow

Designer Kolektyf
Location Krakow, Poland
Client Confidential
Completion 2019
Typeface Archivo
Function Living

The intention of the signage on the residential estate was to correspond with the minimalist design of the building and the black and white interior and façade. Large typography was combined with openwork graphic elements. The synergy of contrast and simplicity makes the signage clear and easy to read. Large, black signs are clearly visible in all parts of the garage. To give the building's façade a wooden feel, white plywood numbers were used to indicate the numbers of the floors and apartments.

↖ Big garage markings
← Contrast marking the exit from the garage level to the elevator

↑ Directional signage at street level
← Pictograms

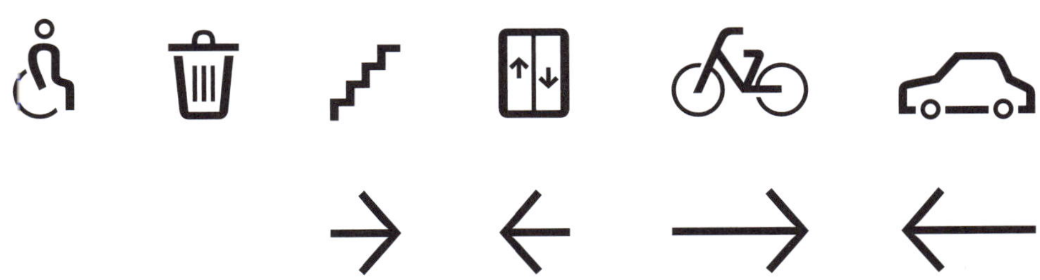

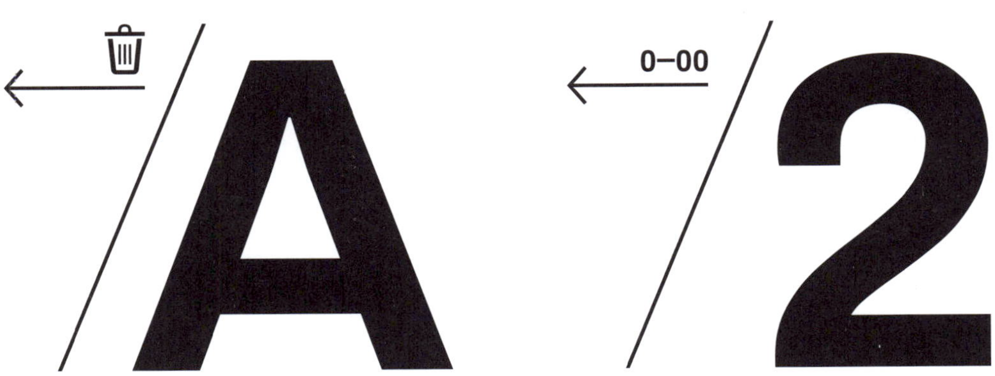

↑ Wall mark of the floor number in the staircase

↓ Detail of signage of the level number

→ View of the levels signage from outside the building
↓ Spacial organization of garage level markings
↘ Entire wall signage of garage level

JAMES SIMON GALERIE
GEÖFFNET
OPEN
JAMES-SIMON-GALERIE

Tickets
ALTES MUSEUM
Audioguide
Information
Tickets
Tickets
Audioguide
PERGAMON MUSEUM

Museumsinsel Berlin
James-Simon-Galerie

Designer polyform – planen und gestalten
Location Berlin, Germany
Client Bundesamt für Bauwesen und Raumordnung (BBR)
Completion 2019
Architect David Chipperfield Architects
Typeface MI Grotesk with pictograms
Function Museum & exhibition space

In the summer of 2019, the James Simon Gallery was opened as a new entrance building on the Museum Island Berlin. In this distribution building visitors can expect to find clearly visible and easily recognizable routing to the service facilities and to the highlights of the Pergamon Museum and the Neues Museum. All information was placed in large format, strikingly and clearly above head height. The needs of visually impaired people were taken into account when determining the sizes and contrast ratios. The majority of the guidance system was designed with direct wall lettering, and different technologies were used depending on the font size and background. Large-format media walls placed above the counters were planned to display digital visitor information.

↖ Staircase with façade banner
← Signpost

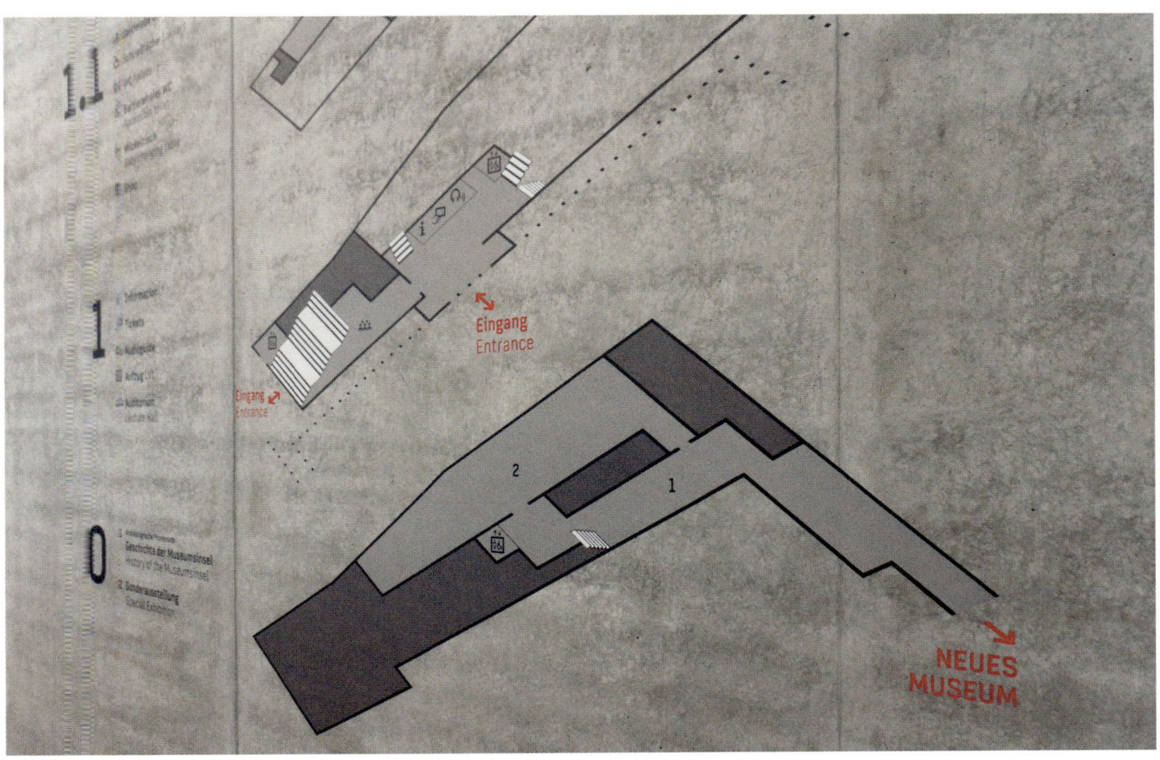

↑ Pictograms
← Floor plan on the wall

↑ Information and signposts at the elevator
↓ Signposting shop

→ Signpost and media wall on second floor
↘ Media wall at the group counter on second floor

Auditorium
Sonderausstellung
Special Exhibition
Archäologische Promenade
Geschichte der Museumsinsel
History of the Museumsinsel
NEUES MUSEUM

GUIDED TOURS
Book your next guided tour online!
SHOPPING 2.0
Visit our museum's shop online!
Groups
registration
PUBLIC GUIDED TOURS ON SATURDAYS 11.30 AND 14.00 HRS
Take Five - Highlights
AUDIO GUIDE
Audio guides in up to 11 languages
information
tickets
Die Museumsinsel Berlin - UNESCO Weltkulturerbe
Information
Gruppen
Groups

INSELHALLE

Inselhalle Lindau

Designer Sägenvier DesignKommunikation
Location Lindau (Lake Constance), Germany
Client Auer Weber
Completion 2018
Architect Auer Weber
Product designer Raunjak Intermedias
Typeface GT Pressura
Function Public

The Inselhalle Lindau with an adjoining multi-story car park is a congress and event location situated between Lake Constance and the historic old town of the island. Sägenvier's orientation system combines signage with scenography: Formally the design reflects the architecture of Auer Weber, narratively it associates the topography of Lindau.
The design moves in exchange with the ensemble: The geometrically typography, derived from the roof, elegantly harmonizes with the used materials. In the tarnish protection, it quotes the rhythm of the façade, in the parking garage the visitors are guided by using copper-colored graphics. Sägenvier developed the typography, a template font, from the drone perspective of the angular roof surface geometry. The halls 1, 2, and 3 form the core of the new Inselhalle.

← Entrance
↙ Typography
↑ Wardrobe

The typography is milled out of oak panels and completed with LED light that is highlighted if a specific room is to be displayed. In the large foyer, a staircase leads down to the lounge, conference rooms, and wardrobe in the basement.
The ceiling surface is used to signalize the way clearly – as a kind of urban guiding fresco across the heads of the visitors. Copper shades on concrete for wall paintings, lettering, and floor markings give the strict functionality a warm touch.
The naive wall paintings illustrate, scenographically ascending, the island position of Lindau: Underwater world/downstairs, Navigation/ground floor, Treetops/first floor, Roofs/second floor and Sky/third floor. Since 1951, the annual Nobel Laureate Conference has been an international forum for scientific exchange. The roof light trapeze in the foyer serves to document and acknowledge excellent researchers. Their names read like a who's who of personalities from medicine, physics, and chemistry.

↖ Foyer
← Parking garage upper floor 2
↑ Typography
↓ Infographic

→ Room labeling
↓ Roof light trapeze
↘ Parking garage upper floor 3

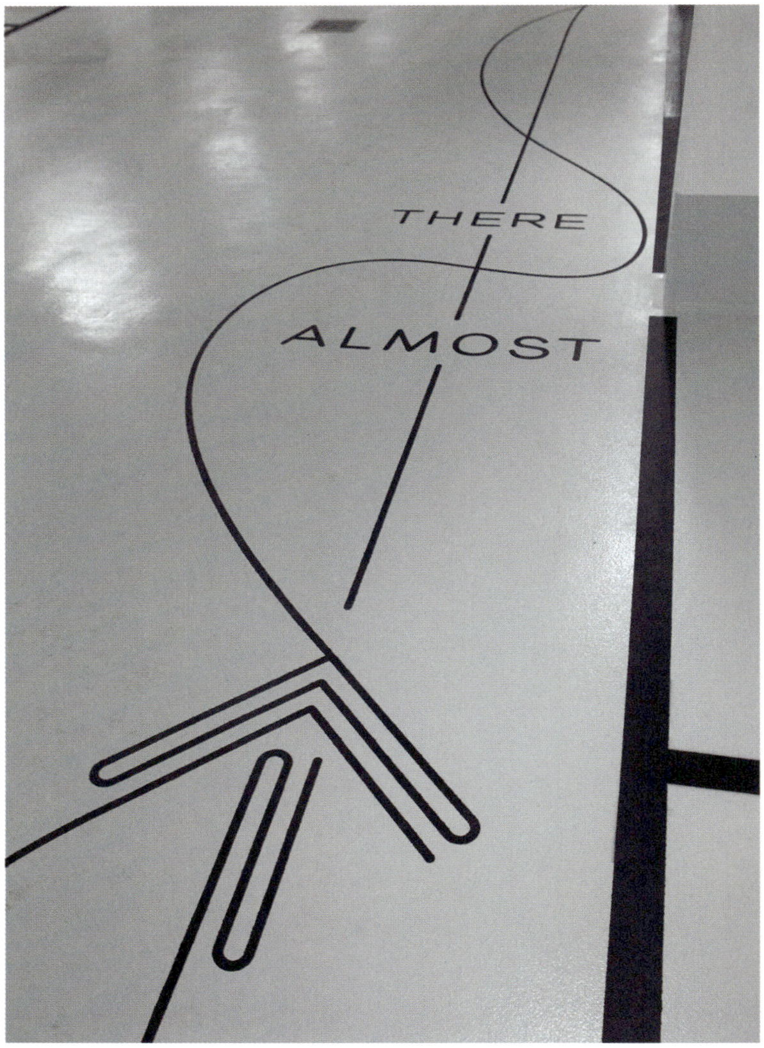

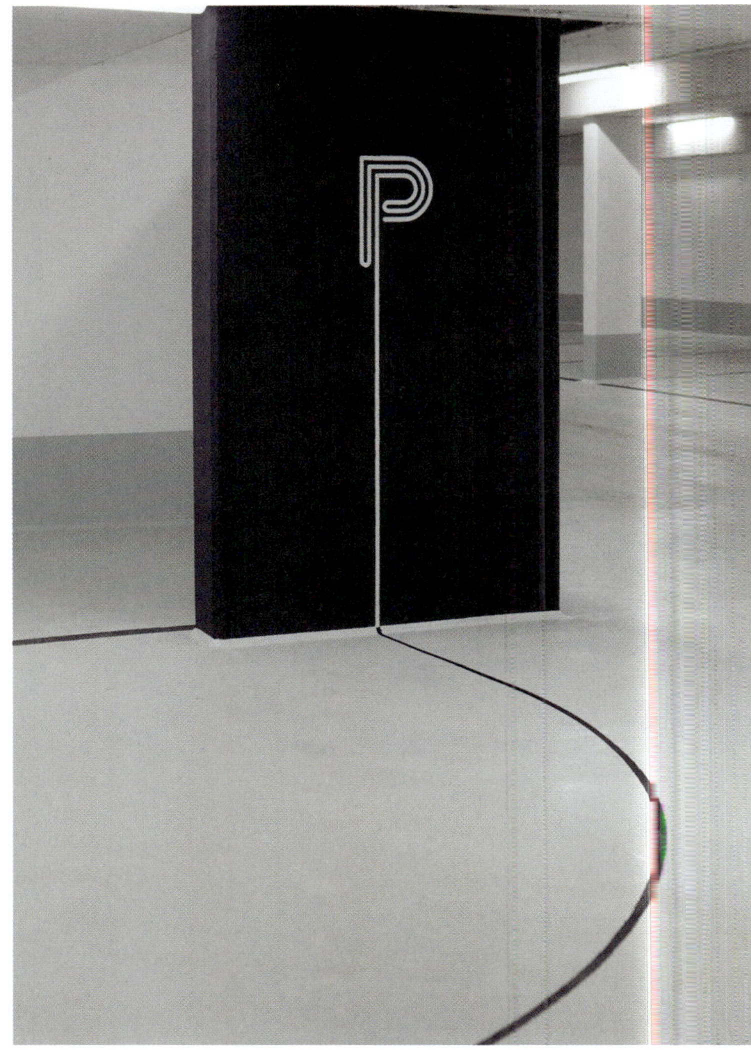

Soulmade Wayfinding System

↖ Guiding line with inscription
↓ Parking spaces for electric cars
↑ Guiding line on the wall and on the floor
↗ Map of the surroundings
→ Guiding line with inscription

<u>Designer</u> Benedek & Co. Brand & Design
<u>Location</u> Garching bei München, Germany
<u>Client</u> Soulmade Hotel & Co-Living
<u>Typeface</u> Chapeau Regular
<u>Function</u> Hospitality

Taking inspiration from the pre-existing logotype of the hotel brand, a modular signage system was developed that includes a typeface and array of icons all based on the logo's appearance. The signet's fluid visual style was applied to walls and floors alike, where the logo's lines flowed all the way from the entrance of the garage to the door of the hotel, changing form and displaying guides.

AIRPORT
(15 MIN)
GARCHINGER SEE
SOULMADE
THERME ERDING
(20 MIN)
LANGWIEDER SEE
THERESIENSTRASSE
UNIVERSITÄT
KÖNIGSPLATZ
ENGLISCHER
GARTEN
ODEONSPLATZ
HAUPTBAHNHOF
KARLSPLATZ
STACHUS
LEHEL
SENDLINGER TOR
STARNBERGER SEE
(45 MIN)
ISAR
OVERVIEW
C1 ALTSTADT-LEHEL
C2 LUDWIGS-ISARVORSTADT
C3 MAXVORSTADT
01 FRAUENKIRCHE
02 MARIENPLATZ
03 MUSEUMSVIERTEL
04 BAYERISCHE STAATSOPER
05 MÜNCHNER RESIDENZ
06 ODEONSPLATZ
07 EISBACH
08 ALTER PETER
09 CHINESISCHER TURM
10 DEUTSCHES MUSEUM
11 THERESIENWIESE
12 OLYMPIAPARK
13 ZOO HELLABRUNN
14 FC BAYERN
15 M.O.C.
16 SCHLOSS SCHLEISSHEIM
17 MESSE RIEM
18 BMW MUSEUM
19 SCHLOSS NYMPHENBURG
20 BOTANISCHER GARTEN
21 GOLFCLUB ESCHENRIED
22 WESTPARK
23 ALLIANZ ARENA
LEAVE A NOTE!

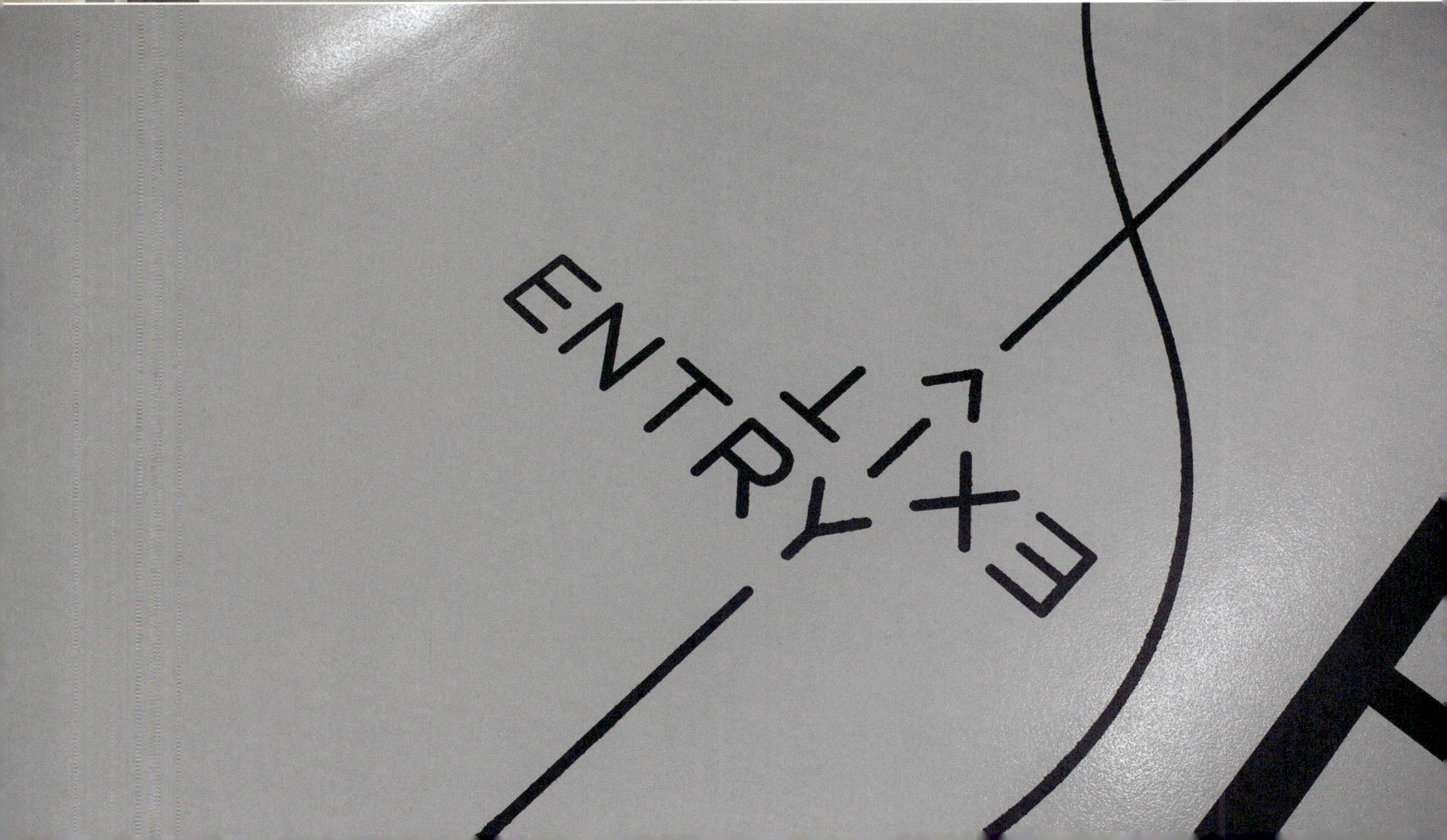
ENTRY
EXIT

FLOOR
4
6
Salon de Parfums
5
Men's Designer Casuals & Outdoor
Ski
Sportswear
Womenswear
Restaurants
4
Childrenswear
Nursery Furniture & Prams
Sweet Street
Toys
Womenswear
Restaurants
3
Bed & Bath
Furniture and Home Accessories
Luxury Linens
Pens, Gifts & Stationery
Technology
Restaurants
2
Books, Cards & Gift Wrap
Harrods Gift Shop
Harrods Luxury Property
Home Decoration
Kitchenware
Pet Accessories
Tableware
Restaurants
ATM
1
Womenswear
Restaurants
G
LG

Harrods – Wayfinding Strategy

Designer Endpoint / Pentagram
Location London, United Kingdom
Client Harrods
Completion 2017
Typeface Caslon Egyptian
Product designer Endpoint / Pentagram
Function Retail

Harrods is a world-class, luxury shopping brand. It's also a huge store – 330 departments spread across a million square feet (90,000 sqm). Such an iconic destination required a success-driven wayfinding solution because customers were easily disorientated within the store. They struggled to find specific products among big-name boutiques. As a result, certain areas of the store were prone to overcrowding and staff would waste time giving directions rather than selling goods.

Working closely with Pentagram Design, Endpoint created a customer-centric wayfinding experience; one that met Harrods' brand values – British heritage, luxury, innovation and sensational – and tastefully reflected the store's art nouveau aesthetic.

← Level 4 totem
↙ Identification sign

↑↑ Identification
↑ Floor directory detail

Endpoint conducted 18 months of research to get some key insights; interviewing staff and customers, analyzing popular areas of the store, and even watching CCTV footage. It became clear that Harrods faced similar navigational challenges to large museums. To mirror this, Endpoint's primary solution was to introduce a simple hall numbering system; one which would maintain the wayfinding experience regardless of space usage, unify digital services and printed guides.

↑ Room identification
↓ Wayfinding sign

→ Stair identification sign
↘ Mini totem

CENTRAL STAIRS

Toilets
Halls 2-5
Champagne Bar
Lifts
Halls 6-17

ALTE PINAKOTHEK

Highlighting the Elegance of the Alte Pinakothek

Designer Sunder-Plassmann & Werner
Location Munich, Germany
Client Bayerische Staatsgemäldesammlung
Completion 2019
Graphic designer Nathalie Nierengarten, Bureau Stabil
Typeface development Typocalypse
Typeface Pinakothek Display
Function Public

The office Sunder-Plassmann & Werner Szenografie developed a new visitor guidance system for the museum Alte Pinakothek in Munich. This emphasizes the simple elegance of the architecture, harmonizes with the different surfaces and picks up the history of the building.
The Alte Pinakothek was built in 1835 by Leo von Klenze and rebuilt in 1957 after its destruction in the Second World War according to the plans of the architect Hans Döllgast. Further renovations and additions followed. The reorganization of the foyer and the design of the exhibition halls by Sunder-Plassmann Architects in 2019 is once again based on Döllgast's elegant architecture.

← Gold letters on the wind screen
↙ The central distribution column in the foyer

↑ Brushed and waxed brass letters on wood

For the new signage system, the Alte Pinakothek received its own typeface, developed on the basis of an unknown typeface design by Döllgast (around 1928), which was found during project research in the archive. Together with the graphic designer Nathalie Nierengarten of the Bureau Stabil and the type designers Typocalypse, a strict and carefully modernized grotesque typeface was created. The brass letters – partially gold-plated – appear haptic, elegant and discreet on the large wall surfaces of the building.
The guidance system covers the entire interior and exterior of the Alte Pinakothek. For the first time, the building also received a lettering at the entrance portal. The new signposts in the parks also refer to the surrounding museum buildings.

ABCDEFGHIJKL
MNOPQRSTUV
WXYZ 12345678
90 ÄÉÜß !?•. ;,*

↑ Entrance to the upper galleries
↓ Brushed and waxed brass letters on painted walls

↑ Gilded brass letters on the rusticated brick wall in the foyer

↑↑ Typeface
→ Lettering above the main entrance

ALTE PINAKOTHEK
BARERSTRASSE
27
ALTE PINAKOTHEK
Öffnungszeiten
Gallery hours
Dienstag
Tuesday
10.00–20.00
Mittwoch–Sonntag
Wednesday–Sunday
10.00–18.00
Montag geschlossen
Monday closed

learning
1.03
studying
researching
1a

intelligent wayfinding

Jackie and Harold Spielman
CHILDREN'S LIBRARY
EXIT

Jackie & Harold Spielman Children's Library

Designer SKOLNICK Architecture + Design Partnership
Location Port Washington, NY, USA
Client Port Washington Public Library
Completion 2018
Contractor Stalco Construction, Inc.
Illustrator Rob Dunlavey
Function Public library

SKOLNICK was engaged to provide interpretive planning, interior architectural design, and exhibit and graphic design services for the renovation of the Children's Library at Port Washington Public Library, which serves children from birth to tweens. The focal point of the design incorporates an over-arching tree motif and a vibrantly colored, leaf-inspired wayfinding system that assists young visitors in self-guided discovery and learning. Each leaf displays an inspirational word representing the theme of its area: Play (early childhood), Imagine (story corner), Think (quiet study), Create (maker's place), Connect (media area). The space, which incorporates multimedia elements and the latest in interactive technology, also includes inviting seating opportunities throughout for parents and caregivers. The overall experience of the redesigned Children's Library is one of welcome, whimsy, discovery, and a celebration of the joy of learning.

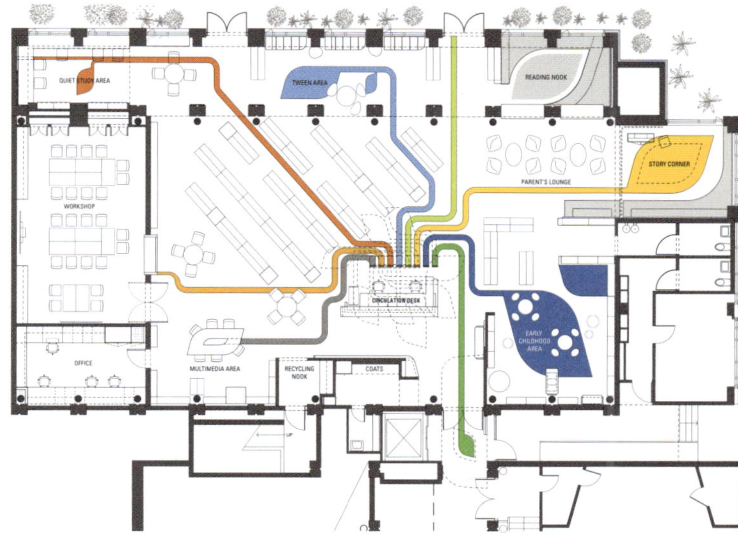

← Leaf-inspired entryway
↓ Tree of knowledge wayfinding graphics

↑↑ Floor plan
↑ North wall graphics

↑ Custom window seat listening stations

↓ Green multimedia table and yellow display case

↑ Colorful graphics roots from the central form seating tree structure

→ Quiet study area with views into the adjacent children's garden

Reading a book is like
looking through a window!
–Zetta Hupf

MITTELBAU
3 313–319, 328–331
2 212–214, 224–234
Aula, Konzilzimmer
Professorenzimmer
Begegnungszimmer
Dezernat 1 (Hofanbau)
1 108–110, 120–133
Rektor, Kanzler
Prorektoren (Hofanbau)
Das Erdgeschoss Mittelbau (012–034) erreichen Sie über den Rechten Flügel

321
322
320
325
323

Inclusion Guidance System

Designer inkl. Design
Location Rostock, Germany
Client University of Rostock
Completion 2013
Interior design Büro Baldauf
Function Education

The main building of the University of Rostock has four historical building parts, which are connected by countless stairs, elevators and crossings. To find one's way was a difficult undertaking for students and teaching staff. The office inkl. Design, as a specialist agency for inclusive design, together with the interior designers Büro Baldauf Schwerin, achieved a targeted orientation with the new guidance system, which the university also opens up to people with disabilities.
Clear color coding of the building sections in accordance with standards; easily legible lettering in accordance with DIN; high contrasts and pictograms that are also easily recognizable for people with visual impairments; correct mounting heights as an aid for people in wheelchairs were included in the design and implementation of the inclusive guidance system. Signs and plans with information in Braille and with tactile floor plans enable even blind people to navigate the campus completely independently.

↖ Tactile floor plan with Braille and profile lettering
← Self-standing indoor signpost
→ Tactile floor plan
↘ Pictogram barrier-free toilet
↓ Tactile doorplate with Braille and profile lettering

↑ Plan with location of the room numbers in the different parts of the building

↓ Wall-mounted orientation board with tactile floor plan

↓ Tactile handrail signage with profile and Braille

→ Freestanding floor signpost with profile and Braille lettering and tactile floor plan

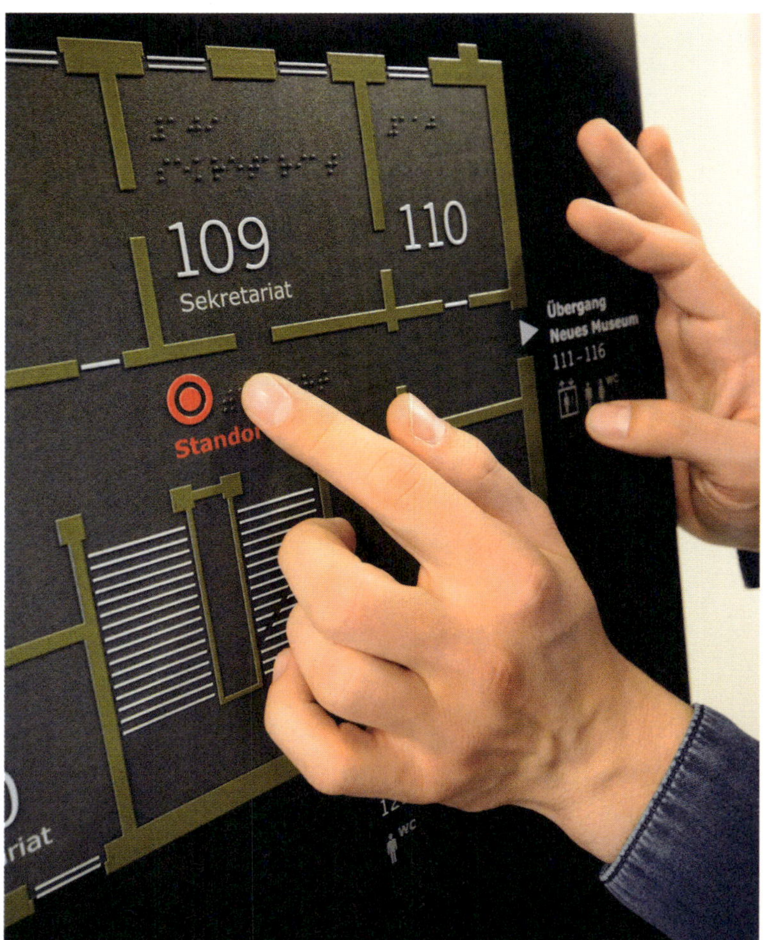

1
HOFANBAU
121 - 128
Prorektoren
124
125
126
122
121
127
128

Wadawarrung 2

Deakin Downtown

Designer Studio Semaphore
Location Melbourne, Australia
Client Deakin University
Completion 2017
Architect Hassell
Interior designer Hassell
Typeface GT Walsheim
Function University

Semaphore was engaged to provide branding and wayfinding signage for Deakin University's new corporate center in Docklands. The brief called for an integrated and intuitive system that would sit alongside the highly refined finishes and Deakin's eclectic art collection.
The resulting design used a muted color palette of matte black and antique white to provide highly legible messaging without cluttering the interior. Studio Semaphore explored the opportunities presented by new 3D printing techniques, finding a solution using SLS (Selective Laser Sintering) Nylon printing to fabricate each individually modeled letter and pictogram. The signage sits beautifully alongside the stone and timber of the interior and creates a consistent language between the physical and digital signage elements.

← Room identification
↙ Projected amenities sign
↑ 3D-printed typography
↓ Directional sign

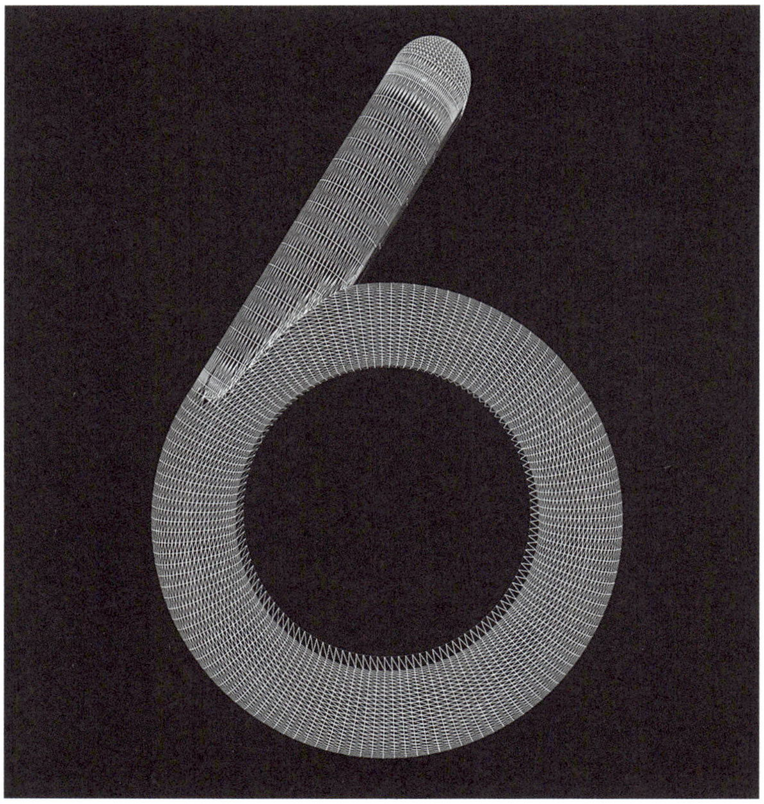

↑ Typography 3D model
↓ Pictograms and arrows

↑ Amenities 3D model

→ Utility room sign

P01 Female

P02 Male

P03 Accessible - Right

P04 Accessible - Left

P05 B+T Female

P06 B+T Male

P07 B+T Accessible

P08 B+T Ambulant Female

P09 B+T Ambulant Female

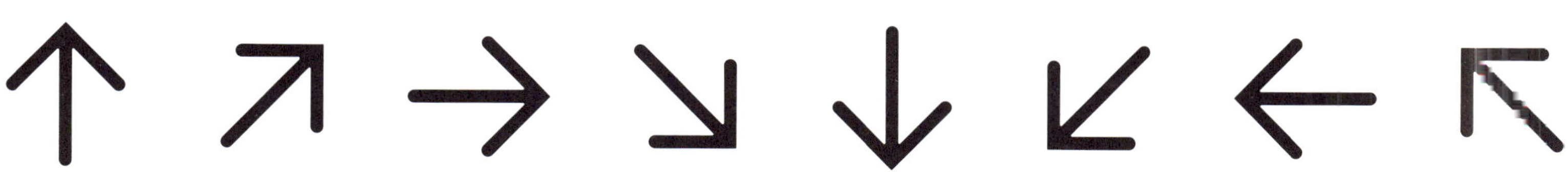

A01 Up/ Straight Ahead

A02 Up to the right/ Turn right ahead

A03 Turn right

A04 Down to the right

A05 Down

A06 Down to the left

A07 Left turn

A08 Up to the left/ Left turn ahead

COMMS

oba next
1
8 kantoren | offices
zalen 8.1 - 8.3 | rooms 8.1 - 8.3
7 restaurant
babel
uitkijkpunt | viewpoint
babyverschoning | baby change
toilet
6 theater, forum & congres
collectie 300-499 | collection 300-499
• maatschappij & politiek | society & politics
oba theater | oba theatre
oba congres | oba congress
oba forum | oba forum
zalen 6.1 - 6.6 | rooms 6.1 - 6.6
toilet
5 studie | study
collectie 500-699 | collection 500-699
• natuur & techniek | nature & science
huis van alle talen 5 | house of all languages 5
leef en leerpunt
zalen 5.1 - 5.2 | rooms 5.1 - 5.2
service & info
4 kunst & media | art & media
collectie 700-799 | collection 700-799
• kunst, muziek, dvd's & cd's | art, music, dvd's & cd's
huis van alle talen 4 | house of all languages 4
zalen 4.1 - 4.2 | rooms 4.1 - 4.2
filmzone | movie zone
luisterzone | audio zone
3 amsterdam
collectie 000-299 en 900-999 | collection 000-299 and 900-999
• geschiedenis & reizen | history & travel
• amsterdam collectie | amsterdam collection
huis van alle talen 3 | house of all languages 3
• franstalige literatuur | french literature
• collectie descartes | descartes collection
ihlia lgbt heritage
spinoza centrum | spinoza centre
zalen 3.1 - 3.2 | rooms 3.1 - 3.2
2 literatuur | literature
collectie 800-889 | collection 800-889
• romans, poezië & strips | novels, poetry & comic books
• collectie jongeren (12-19 jaar) | junior collection (age 12-19)
huis van alle talen 2 | house of all languages 2
• engelstalige literatuur | english literature
ronde zaal | circle room
zalen 2.1 - 2.2 | rooms 2.1 - 2.2
service & info
1 oba next
M café & expo
kranten & tijdschriften | newspapers & magazines
oba expo
galerij | gallery
oba café
toilet
0 entree | entrance
terugbrengen & lenen | return & borrow
reserveringen | reservations
service & info
uitgang | exit
-1 jeugd | junior
jeugd collectie (0-12 jaar) | junior collection (age 0-12)
junior theater | junior theatre
maakplaats | makerspace

Amsterdam Public Library

Designer Studiostaak
Producer Van Beem & Van Haagen
Location Amsterdam, the Netherlands
Client Stichting Openbare Bibliotheek Amsterdam
Completion 2019
Architect Jo Coenen Architect & Urbanist
Pictogram designer MASI
Typeface Avenir
Function Public library

The Amsterdam Public Library (Openbare Bibliotheek Amsterdam, OBA Oosterdok) is the biggest library of the Netherlands. The building has 13 levels and 24,000 square meters filled with books, two theaters, a congress center, a restaurant, a bar, several exposition spaces and a beautiful children's department. The library is designed and recently renovated (2017–2019) by Jo Coenen Architect & Urbanist. The new wayfinding system by Studiostaak makes it possible to easily find all destinations: from a popular theater performance to a single rare book. Next to a general wayfinding system a more playful and intuitive system is designed for the library's junior department. Books are not devided into sections of age, but into worlds of interest: adventure, dreams, playing outside, comics, and so on.

← Totem at OBA next department

↑ Totem at main entrance
↓ Pictograms

speelweide

strips
strips

← Section "play meadow" at OBA junior
↙ Comic section at OBA junior
→ Section "playing outside" at OBA junior
↓ Pictograms junior set

Selbstlernbereich D140
PR-Wiss D132 – D134
Hochschulbibliothek D118 – D128
Büros
BAU D117 – D138
Selbstlernbereich
Büro

FHZ
Orientation System

Designer 22quadrat
Location Münster, Germany
Client Fachhochschule Münster
Completion 2017
Typeface Univers LT Std in 45 Light and 65 Bold
Function Education

The task was to develop an orientation and signage system that allows flexible handling of a variety of different building types and at the same time transports the visual identity of the Fachhochschule Münster, an arts and crafts university. The result is a modular system of varying color fields that nestle up against the architecture like a light veil, set into the corners of the room and give the rooms a clear structure. A particular requirement in the FHZ building was to enliven the monotony of the long corridors, to create stops that allow the eye and the mind to grasp the spatial dimension and allow intuitive orientation. The visual intensity of the graphic work in the FHZ was therefore specially designed for this location. The graphic system is also designed for other buildings with a different character. The design of the colored areas is primarily based on the square, its expressiveness is increased or decreased depending on the type of building and its purpose of use.

↖ Three-dimensional floor number
← Modular system of varying color fields

↑ Room labeling as a visual breakpoint
← Color surface connects walls with floor, ceiling and doors

↑ Building overview in the staircase center
← Color fields that blend into the corners of the room

↓ Typographic solutions within the building overview

→ Oversized building number on outer façade
↓ Modular system of varying color fields

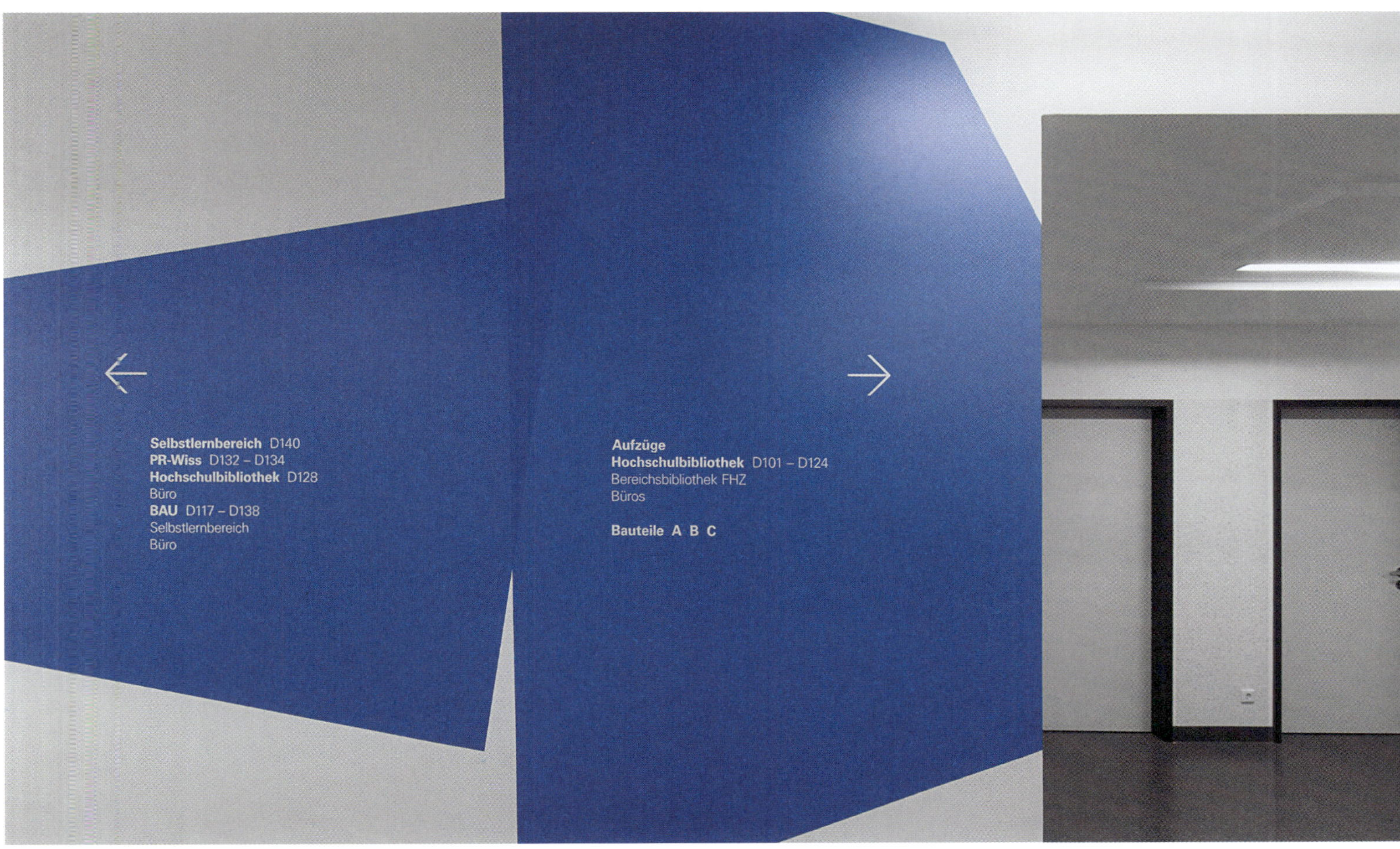

2. 12

St Dominic's International School

Designer P-06 Atelier
Creative director Pedro Anjos
Location Cascais, Portugal
Client St Dominic's International School
Completion 2019
Typeface Diverse, serif and sans serif
Function Education

P-06 Atelier designed the new signage project for a new building extension for the St Dominic's College, an international school in S. Domingos de Rana – Portugal. The building is built with prefabricated solutions showing intentionally the technical installations in strong visual layouts. The signage project proposes a large scale graphic intervention to dilute the strong architectural solutions, creating an animated environment with a school theme. The areas of the different classroom types are identified with big scale titles applied over all the existing elements in the walls, covering doors, corners and cables, justifying the strong visual differences of the building materials. The titles assume different types of calligraphy to illustrate the theme of the room, but also to create a study environment with different types of writing, in a school that is international and brings together children with different nationalities. All the applications are made with cutted vinyl technology.

← General view
↓ Room 2 and 3, labo
→ Site and first floor view
↘ Toilets

↖ Directional signs with building numbers
↑ Pictograms

↗ Pylon at the entrance
→ Column with an overview plan

Guidance and Orientation System for the FernUniversität in Hagen

<u>Designer</u> Kuhl|Frenzel
<u>Location</u> Hagen, Germany
<u>Client</u> FernUniversität in Hagen
<u>Completion</u> 2019
<u>Typeface</u> Frutiger Regular, Frutiger Bold
<u>Function</u> Education

Within the context of the last campus expansion, the FernUniversität in Hagen decided to implement an individual guidance and orientation system in order to achieve an identity-building effect, a high recognition value and efficient study conditions. One challenge was that the campus is built on a hill and is not easily accessible from the access points and central points of the campus. In order to achieve a better overview, the development was conceptually rethought and the buildings and parking spaces were logically redesignated. The design ties in with the established corporate design of the university by picking up on the guiding elements the rounding of the signet motif in the form of rounded corners, the color scheme and the Frutiger font. The system is composed of welcoming, overview-creating, directional and characteristic elements in the exterior and interior, distributed throughout the entire campus. Aspects of visual accessibility as well as the relevant DIN specifications were already taken into account during the planning of the measures, including the choice of font sizes and the high-contrast display. One building has already been upgraded to be barrier-free.

FernUniversität in Hagen

FernUniversität in Hagen
Campus Übersichtsplan

↑ Environment model
← Column in front of the main entrance to the building

↓ Barrier-free building 5

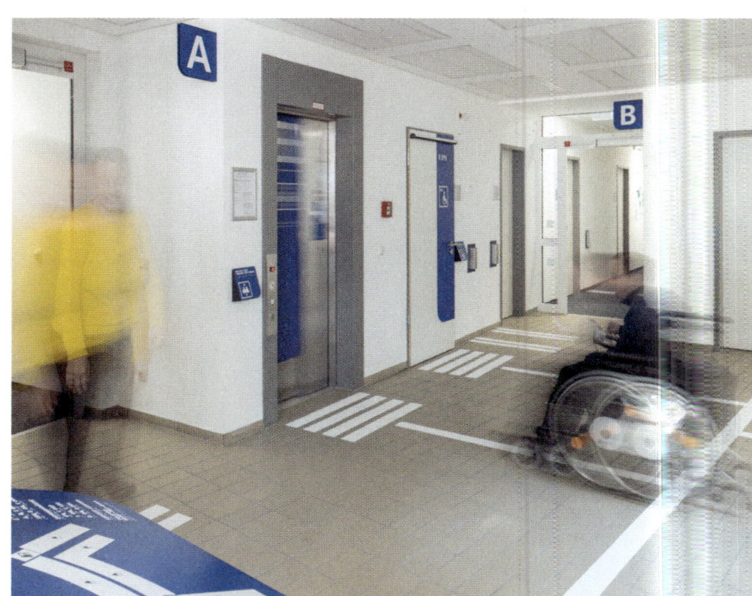

→ Floor plans
↓ Elevators with large colored foil

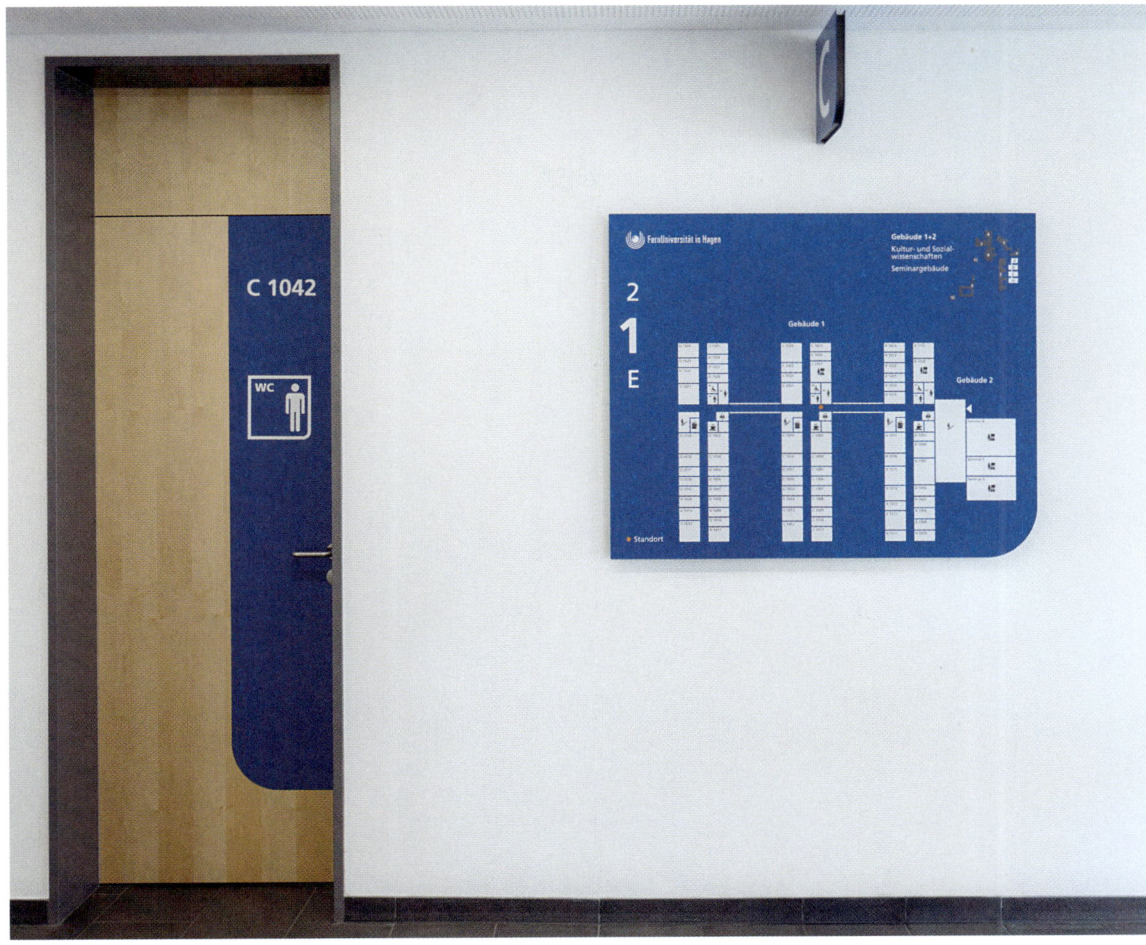

BESPRECHUNGSRÄUME

Seminarräume A–E
Catering

Deutsches Biomasse-forschungszentrum, DFBZ

Designer Form & Fokus
Location Leipzig, Germany
Client Staatsbetrieb Sächsisches Immobilien- und Baumanagement, Niederlassung Leipzig I
Completion 2019
Architect Schulz und Schulz Architekten
Typeface Replica
Function Research

The German Biomass Research Center in Leipzig is an important research institution for the development and use of renewable energies. With the two new buildings, a pilot plant and an office building, the working and research conditions have been expanded and optimized. The architectural design aims at a holistic approach to sustainable construction with the focus on energy efficiency, use of ecological building materials, quality of use and user acceptance. Accordingly, the control system was also designed to meet the demands of research and development. The design form is to be understood analogously to the procedures for the efficient and sustainable use of solid, liquid and gaseous bioenergy sources. Representing the diversity of biomass as a compressed energy source, all information carriers are milled from OSB coarse chipboard from sustainable forestry. The desired identity-forming effect is created by the combination of materiality, individual, untreated surface structures, filigree milling forms and typeface. The individual, three-dimensional information elements include elevator overviews, floor markings, directional arrows, movable walls, destination confirmations and spatial numerals. All interchangeable carriers are formed by combining filigree plug-in strips with individually incorporated acrylic glass plates for paper inserts.

← Destination confirmation sign
↙ Signposting, arrow with variable plate

↑ Signposting and elevator

← Detail destination confirmation sign

3

1.129

1.134
1.152

←← Elevator overview, number
← Doorplate kitchenette
→ Room number copy room

← Pictograms next to doors
→ Doorplate cleaning room

AUDITORIO
CENTRO DE INNOVACION UC
ANACLETO ANGELINI
INSPIRAR
CONECTAR
Y ORQUESTAR
LA INNOVACIÓN
10 pisos, 9.000 m² en un espacio
para promover una cultura pro
innovación y emprendimiento
centrodeinnovacion@uc.cl • (56-2) 2 354 2250

3

PUC Center for Innovation

Designer Wayfinding Consultores
Location Santiago de Chile, Chile
Client Pontificia Universidad Católica
Completion 2016
Architect Elemental
Typeface Geogrotesque
Function University

The Center for Innovation Anacleto Angelini at the Pontificia Universidad Católica (PUC) aims to provide a link between academic research and the private sector, with the hope of transforming well-conceived research into public policies that improve the living conditions of Chileans. Created in 2016 by renowned Pritzker-winning architect Alejandro Aravena, this institution was designed as a regular prism – a cube – being dissected by an unknown force: a cube in motion.
Using this powerful metaphor as an starting point, Wayfinding Consultores developed a series of small cube-inspired environmental graphic interventions in the building, which co-exist with large-scale interventions for the atrium. In order to respond to the center's changing events, they designed a series of small panels where information printed by standard printers is inserted, and which permit managers to provide information about news and daily changes in the schedule.

← Large-scale interventions in the atrium
↙ Floor numbers on glass

↑↑ Pictograms
↑ General information
↓ Panels to display standard print-outs

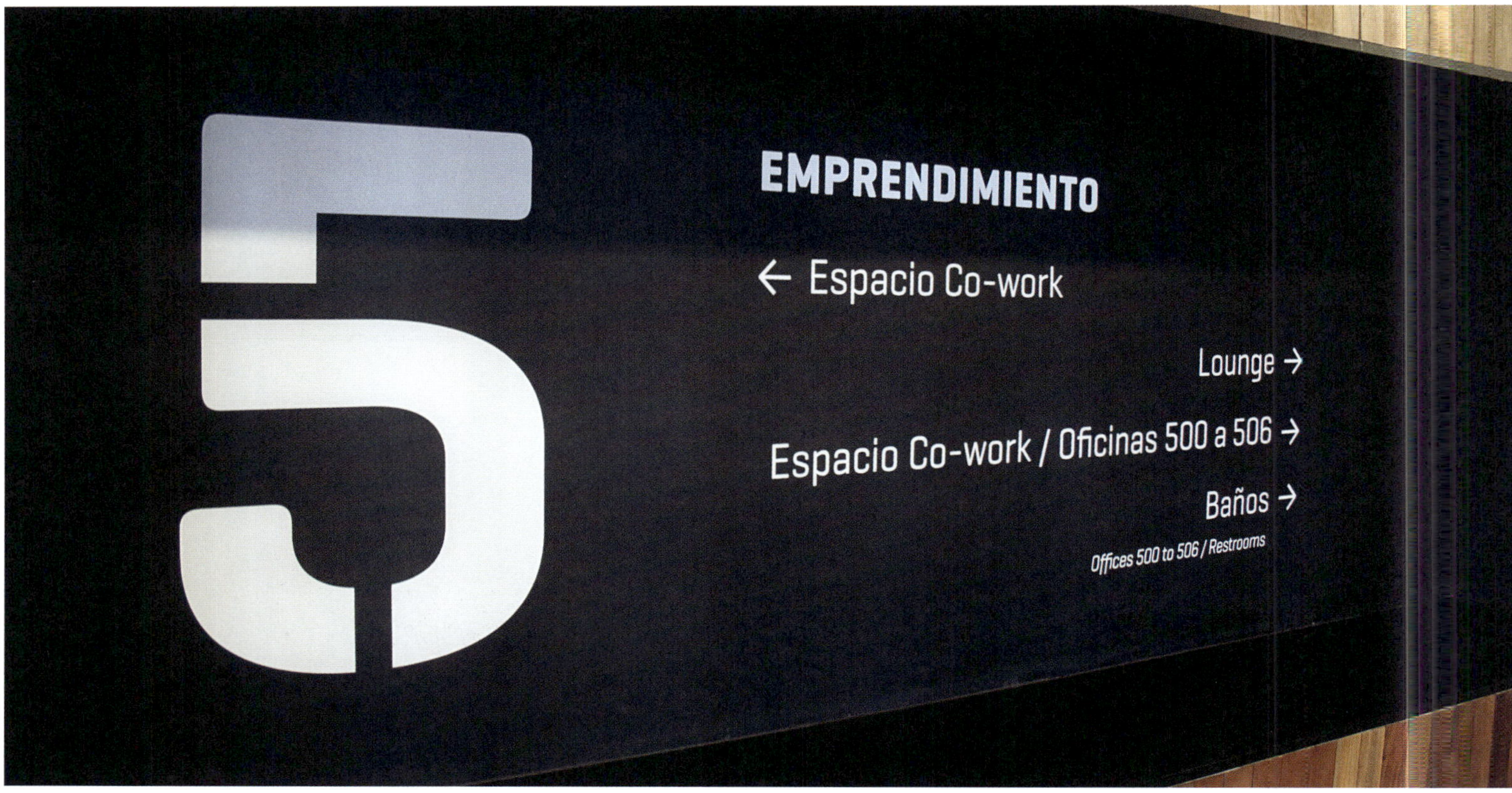

↑ Orientation by numbers
and arrows
↓ Development out of cubes

→ Large floor number painted
on the concrete wall

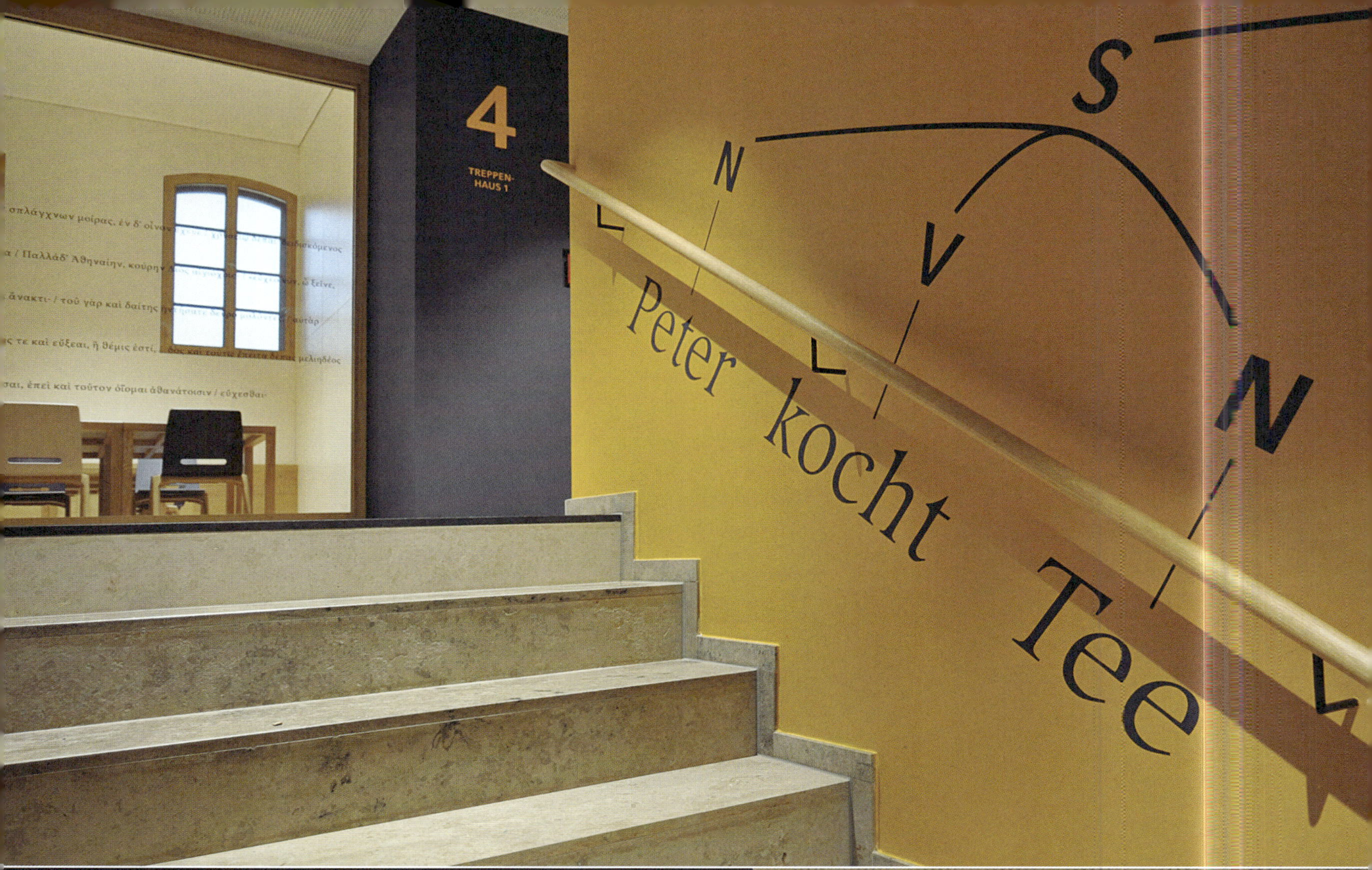
4
TREPPEN-
HAUS 1
S
N
V
N
Peter kocht Tee

D
NP
S
N
VP
Das Buch hilft.

Philologicum – Subject Library LMU Munich

Designer Studio Eva Plass with Benedikt Haid
Location Munich, Germany
Client Staatliches Bauamt München 2
Completion 2019
Architect Cukrowicz Nachbaur Architekten
Typeface LMU Compatil
Function Education

Studio Eva Plass developed a signage concept for the new LMU Philologicum library. This concept takes into account the specific user requirements of the new library and also integrates the content context of the specialist library for linguistics with identity-creating signs into the planning. The wayfinding elements are screen-printed directly onto the wooden paneling in the interior rooms and thus integrate harmoniously into the clear architecture of Cukrowicz Nachbaur Architekten. Literature quotations in various languages from books in the library stock are used on glass surfaces in the building. Excerpts from Homer's Odyssey serve as window safety decals on the glass doors of the staircases. In the stairwells, syntax trees from the field of linguistics on the walls support orientation on the way. With single, group and silent study areas, the library is a place that invites people to work, linger, exchange and network.

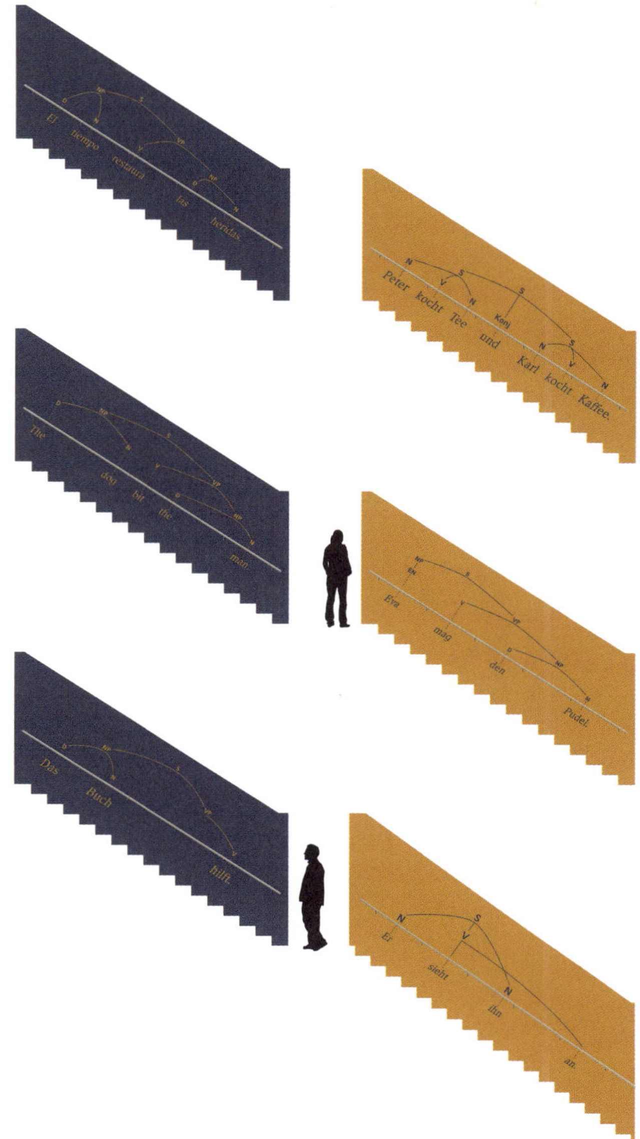

↖ Wall display with linguistic syntax trees (yellow)
← Wall display with linguistic syntax trees (blue)

↑ Staircases concept design
← View into library reading area

→ Wall display with linguistic syntax trees (yellow and blue)
↘ Detail level overview
⇘ Foyer signpost

↑ Group study room
↓ Single study room

beat
bate

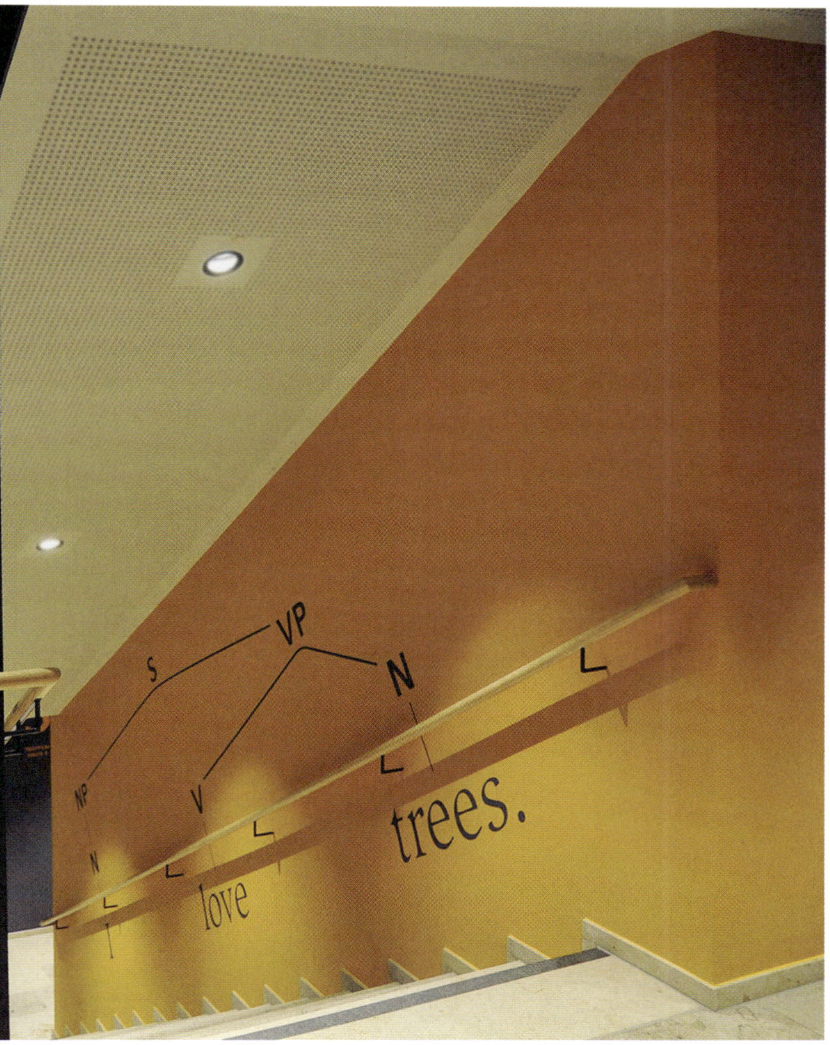
VP
S
N
NP
V
N
I
love
trees.

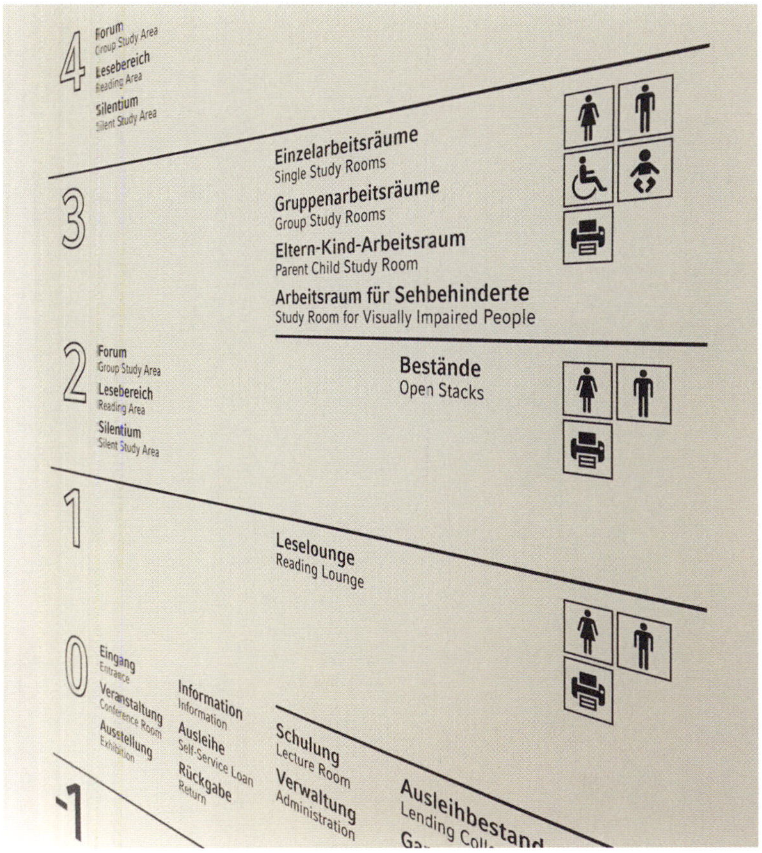
4
Forum
Group Study Area
Lesebereich
Reading Area
Silentium
Silent Study Area
Einzelarbeitsräume
Single Study Rooms
Gruppenarbeitsräume
Group Study Rooms
3
Eltern-Kind-Arbeitsraum
Parent Child Study Room
Arbeitsraum für Sehbehinderte
Study Room for Visually Impaired People
2
Forum
Group Study Area
Lesebereich
Reading Area
Silentium
Silent Study Area
Bestände
Open Stacks
1
Leselounge
Reading Lounge
0
Eingang
Entrance
Veranstaltung
Conference Room
Ausstellung
Exhibition
Information
Information
Ausleihe
Self-Service Loan
Rückgabe
Return
Schulung
Lecture Room
Verwaltung
Administration
Ausleihbestand
-1

working
meeting

business wayfinding

filing

EMRE
GROUP

Emre Group Head Office

Designer Renda Helin Design & Interiors
Location Istanbul, Turkey
Client Emre Group
Completion 2017
Interior designer Renda Helin Design & Interiors
Function Work

The Emre Group, based in Sisli, Istanbul, is established in the construction, tourism and automotive sectors with its visionary approach. The company's vision and innovative perspective is brought to life in the interior design realized by Renda Helin Design & Interiors. The two-story building covers a total area of 220 square meters including the inner courtyard of the garden. The Emre Group has long been active in the construction industry, which constitutes the main concept of the interior design. The moment you enter the building, you notice the nuances that make you feel like you are on a construction site.
The industrial design approach is adopted to represent the building sector, and is reflected above all in the reception and accounts department, the directors' room, the meeting room and the entrance floor, where the shared toilet is located; and is further enhanced by the yellow and black colors, which also represent another reference to the building sector.

← Company logo on glass pane
↙ Yellow-black stripes on the floor

↑ Stairs to upper floor with sign

The material choices were determined by the raw and natural appearance of the building materials, and the indispensable features of a construction atmosphere were highlighted by materials such as raw concrete, epoxy resin, brick, iron profile and metal mesh.
One of the most striking aspects of the project is undoubtedly hidden in the details.
The Lego Movie inspired the design of the meeting room, and the use of the Lego brick and its character is equally emphasized. The main motto of the film, "Grab a hat and let's build something" has become the basic vision and slogan of the company. One part of the meeting table was made from the original Lego brick, while the other part was made with a lighting element specially designed in the shape of a crane.

↑ Staircase upper floor
↓ Upper floor

↑ Meeting room
→ Hallway to the meeting room

GRAB A HAT AND
LET'S
SOMETHING
ROOM

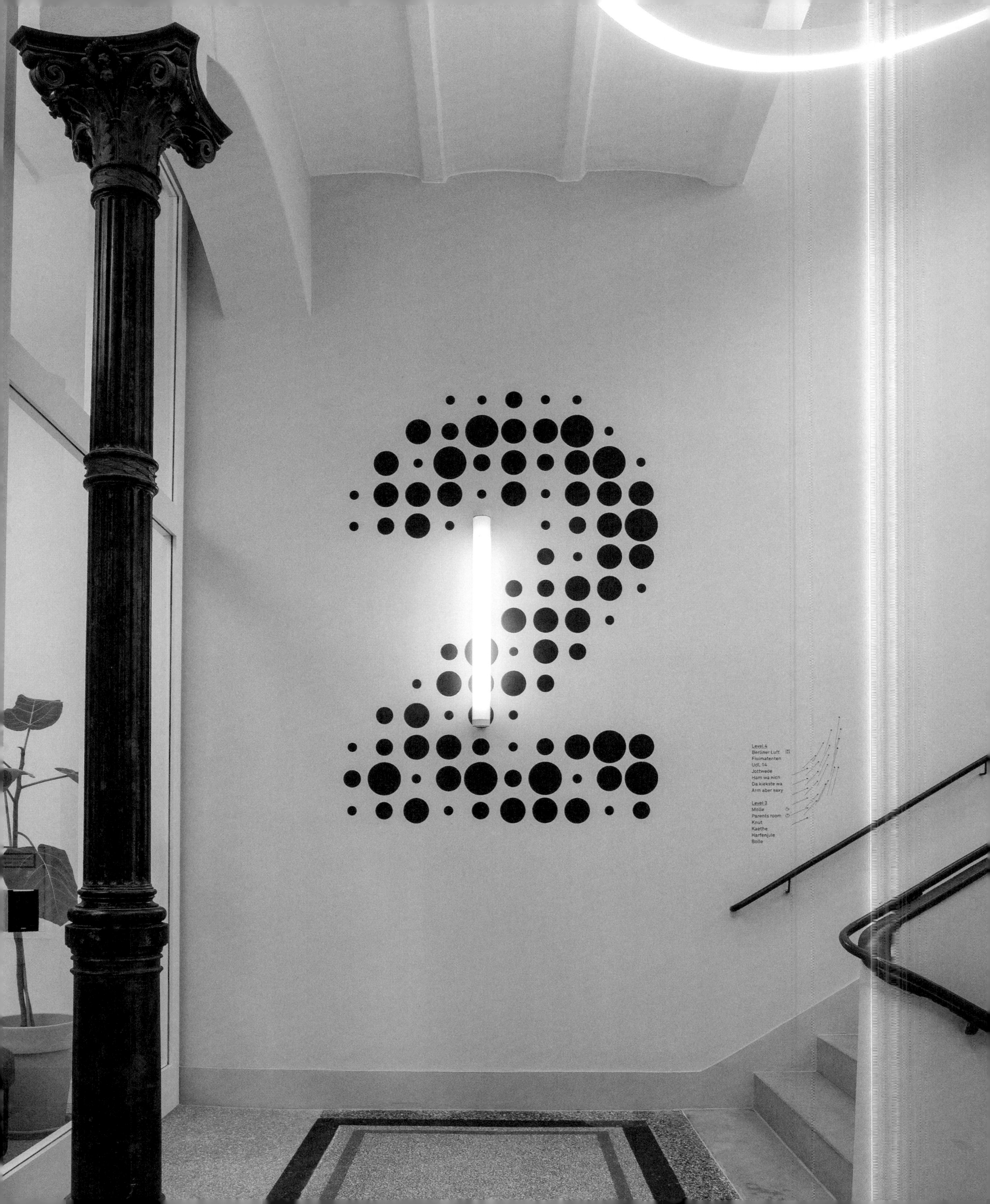
2
Level 4
Berliner Luft
Fisimatenten
UdL 14
Jottwede
Ham wa nich
Da kiekste wa
Arm aber sexy
Level 3
Molle
Parents room
Knut
Kaethe
Harfenjule
Bolle

Google and YouTube Offices in Berlin

Designer SLANG - Studio for graphic design
Location Berlin, Germany
Client Google and YouTube
Completion 2019
Architect Allford Hall Monaghan Morris
Typeface Akkurat
Function Work

SLANG developed, designed and managed the production and installation of wayfinding for the Google and YouTube offices in Berlin. The space is more than 7,000 square meters spread over five floors of a listed building built in 1883 as a women's hospital. To reflect the various types of spaces in the building, the design is based on balancing uniformity of color and a multiplicity of design, forms, and materials. Each floor has an individually designed floor number. Various methods of orientation design were also tested and mixed, such as neon lights and manually painted walls.

↑ Painted floor number
↓ Paint and vinyl directional signage

← Painted floor number, vinyl directional signage

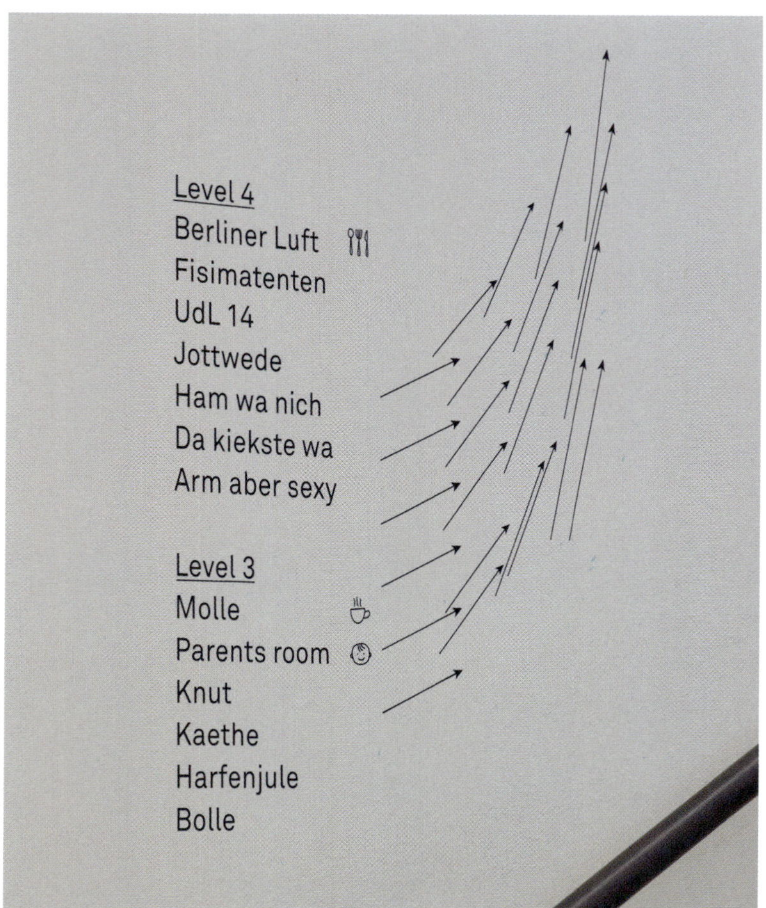

↑ Floor number and directory, MDF and neon

← Vinyl directional signage

↓ Direct print on MDF directional sign

→ Direct print on MDF directional signs
↓ Paint and vinyl directional signage
↘ Vinyl floor number

Châteauform' City Paris Les Puces

↖ Directional signage
↑↑ Decorative wall

↑ Pictograms
↗ Wayfinding system
→ Directional signage with arrow

Designer La Letterie
Location Saint-Ouen, France
Client Châteauform'
Completion 2019
Product designer Marlène Fortanier
Typeface Orator STD - deformed and extra width
Function Work

Châteauform' Paris Les Puces welcomes business meetings and individual visitors. The building is designed around the concept of movement; the meeting rooms are all named according to this concept. The goal in creating the signs was to effortlessly blend in with the building's theme. In order to do this, the designers played around with the width of words by stretching and contracting certain letters thus creating a dance within the words themselves. The horizontal and vertical signs work with hallway and door angles and other building specificities to emphasize not only movement, but the idea of dynamism. The windows design is directly inspired by Rudolph Laban's geometric notation symbols, which are graphic representations of human body positions and movements.

This signage was designed on illustrator but La Letterie chose a block type well adapted to the brush as the whole project was hand-painted.

RION
HYPÉRION
PIXEL

LES MARÉES
JET STREAM
ZÉPHYR

>>> TURM OST >>> TOWER EAST >>>
>>> PARKING LEVELS >>> PARKEBENEN
Exit
Exit

HypoVereinsbank Building Wayfinding System

<u>Designer</u> büro uebele visuelle kommunikation
<u>Location</u> Stuttgart, Germany
<u>Client</u> HypoVereinsbank
<u>Completion</u> 2018
<u>Architect</u> Henn Architekten
<u>Typeface</u> Maison Neue Bold
<u>Function</u> Work

A grid of equilateral triangles forms the basis of the building's architecture: This architectural design feature is the benchmark for the development of all wayfinding applications. The initial public contact is in the reception hall, where visitors and staff are greeted by an apparently floating zigzag ticker strip. LED ticker displays on both sides of the strip issue a constant stream of luminous letters, which shine through the reflections, yielding interesting information. There are three of these ticker displays, 33 meters long in all and, as a bonus, in three languages. As an extra benefit the various arms of the zigzag ticker strips each point in a specific direction, so that the text trends in the right direction, guiding visitors and staff, its content adapted to the length of the arm in each case. This free-floating construction pays off in terms of flexibility, creating the option of mixing wayfinding guidance with ad-hoc realtime announcements. The rest of the system is classically structured,

← Reception hall
↙ Curved glass wall and level signage

↑ Exterior view

with understated lettering providing information on walls in a balanced mix of black and white that matches the architectural context. The same triangle motif is diversified and used in a portfolio of signage applications: For meeting rooms, triangles are added to create surplus privacy. On lift landings the curved glass panels are finished in varying tones of black so that each floor has its own combination of triangles, a subtle identifier code. The secondary signage offers a playful variant on the same theme, with polygonal shapes that match their black or white background, distinguished only by a different gloss finish. At basement level the black-and-white theme continues with large triangle motifs pointing the way on walls and floors. Accents of color are added here and there to alert users to key landmarks: entrances, doors, gateways and signs.

↑ Reception hall with ticker strip
← Reflection on black glass wall and signage
↓ Triangular pattern on the walls

→ Variation of the triangular pattern

↓ Underground car park with graphics

D →
A281–A271
← B C
Saal Ostallgäu
Saal Aggenstein
Saal Wertach I
Saal Wertach II
Ausgang
A
0-4
0-4
EO

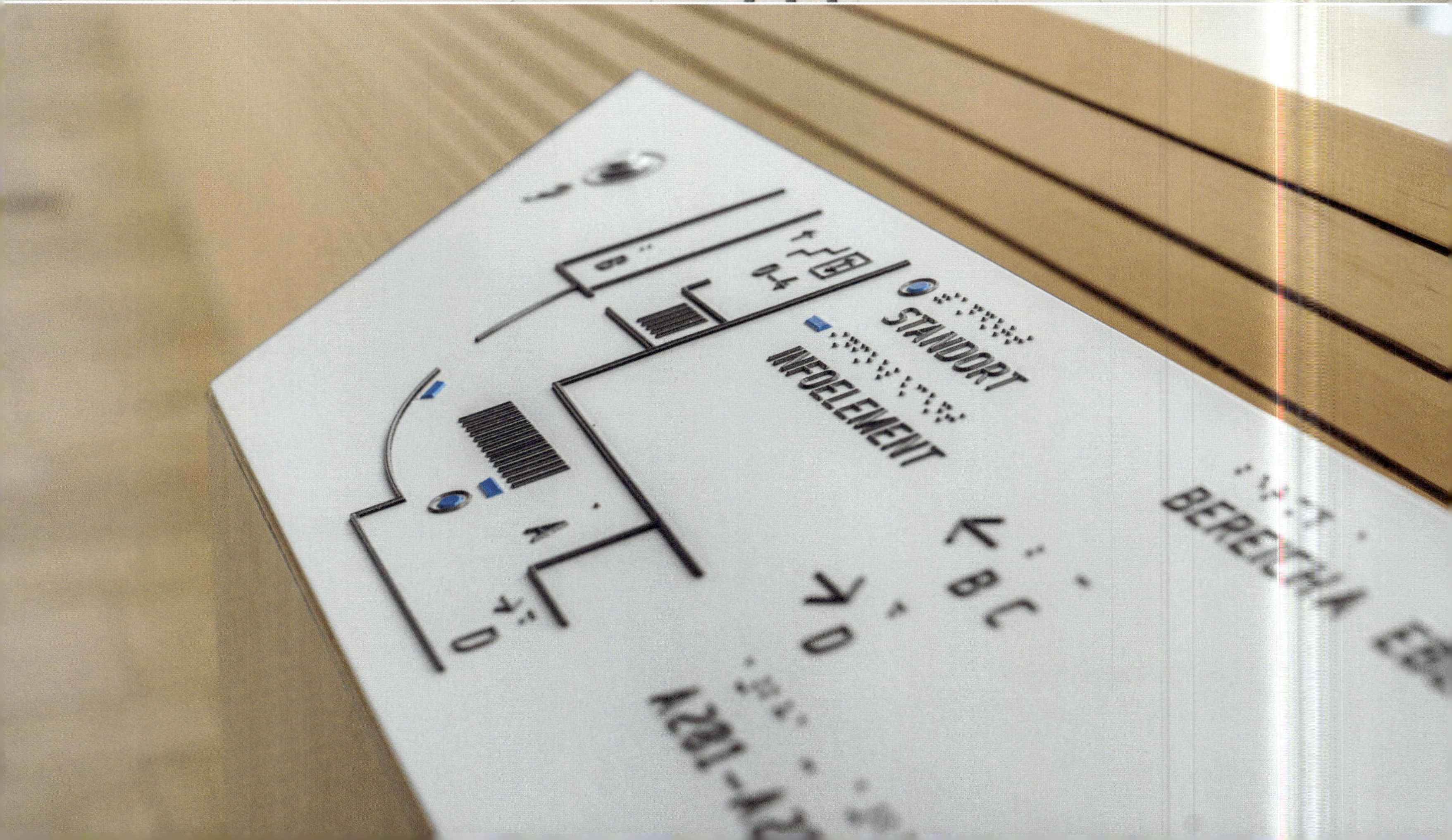
STANDORT
INFOELEMENT
B C
D
A281–A2

Barrier-Free Orientation and Signage System Landratsamt Ostallgäu

Designer designgruppe koop
Location Marktoberdorf, Germany
Client Landratsamt Ostallgäu
Completion 2017
Typeface AF Diwa, Braille
Function Public

The goal was to create a guidance system for people with and without disabilities – with clear instructions for the blind and visually impaired, for wheelchair users, for the deaf and cognitively impaired persons. From the entrance to the room door. The building of the administrative district office has two, three or rather four levels, within which there is a representative area, but mainly long, narrow corridors where there is no possibility to attach information to walls, floors or ceilings.
Out of this situation freestanding elements have been created, which contain all information. In addition, wall variants for the staircases and small door signs on the individual rooms were developed. Further assistance is provided by tactile floor indicators and a tactile model of the building in front of the entrance.

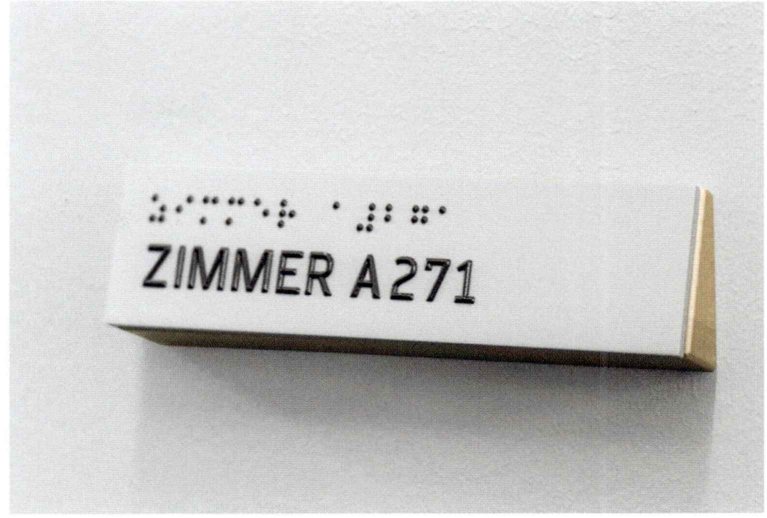

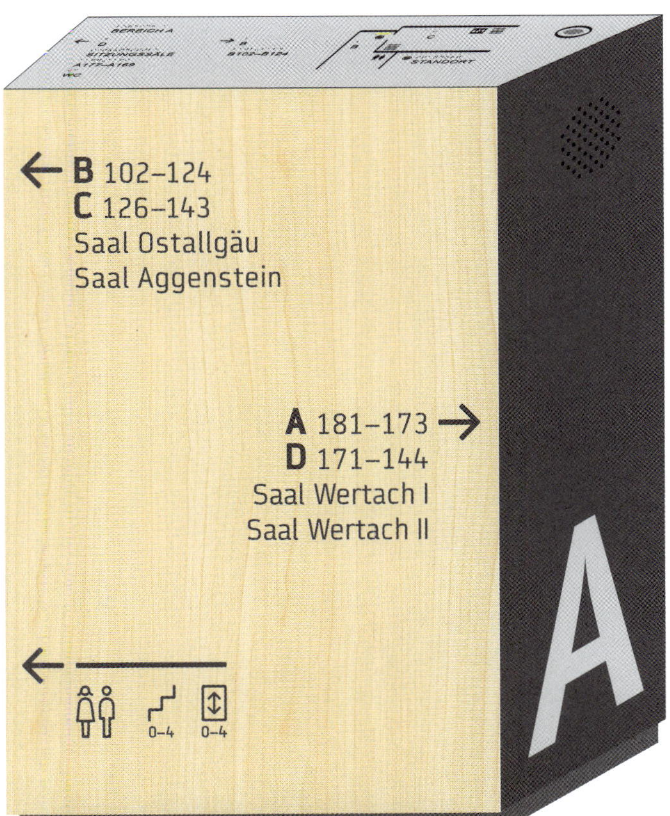

↖ Information element
← Tactile surface of the information element
↙ Visualization of a free-standing information element
↑↑ Button for information read aloud
↑ Small doorplate on an individual room

For accessibility, disabled people normally use the two-senses principle, seeing and feeling. At the correct height and with a 15° inclination, all information is displayed tactilely on the freestanding elements in Braille and pyramid writing. In addition, there are tactile floor plans each in the line of sight. These are also helpful for unimpaired visitors. The special feature: All contents can be read out via a button. An example of barrier-free design that looks good. A pathbreaking realization that allows visitors to the Landratsamt Ostallgäu to move about in a self-determined and non-disrupted way.

↑ Tactile model in front of the entrance

↓ Wall version in the staircase

↓ Freestanding information element

↗ Freestanding information element

→ Icons showing the way to restrooms

←D
A281–A271
BC→
B203–B222

ABCDEFGHIJK
LMNOPQRST
UVWXYZ

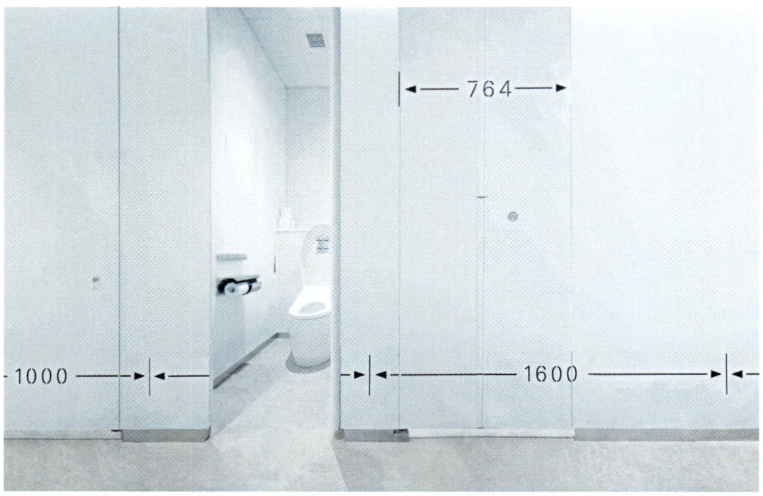

Azusa Sekkei Office Sign

↖↖ Project room numbers
↖ The dimensions are also displayed in the toilet
↓ A corridor with lines like an airport runway
↑↑ Font, remade in 6D
↑ Compass point and diameter
↗ Orientation marking
→ Hall entrance

<u>Designer</u> 6D-K
<u>Location</u> Tokyo, Japan
<u>Client</u> Azusa Sekkei Co.
<u>Completion</u> 2019
<u>Typeface</u> Univers Stencil Light remade in 6D
<u>Function</u> Work

A sign plan for a new office of Japan's leading architecture design firm. The signs are designed pieces of information, so those not in the know may assume that the numbers on the floor and on the wall are merely decoration, but each number and each line plays a much more important role than just conveying accurate information. The office occupies an entire floor of a warehouse, a massive space of six meters tall, and within it are signs to show by meters the distance from the reception, height from floor to doorknob, door width, directions, and so forth. This approach helps those hundreds of architects who work in this office to get dimensions imprinted in their subconsciousness through spontaneous contact.

D2
E1

AZS HALL
1000
2000
1000

Guidance System SOKA-DACH

Designer studio kw. kommunikationsdesign
Location Wiesbaden, Germany
Client Sozialkassen des Dachdeckerhandwerks SOKA-DACH
Completion 2019
Typeface Neusa Next
Function Work

With the relocation of the social security benefits office of the roofers (SOKA-DACH in short) to a new main building, studio kw. kommunikationsdesign was commissioned to plan a new guidance and orientation system. The functional requirements were legibility and presence. The typography is very fine and simple. It follows a strict, diagram-like approach.
To ensure that the lettering fits better into the architecture, it was applied directly to the wall and supplemented by three-dimensional elements in the overviews.
The strict approach of the typography was contrasted with large spacious floor numbers. These consist of painted aluminum, covered on the back with blue foil and mounted at a distance from the wall. This creates a bluish rear light effect, which in turn refers to the corporate color of the SOKA-DACH.
In order to refer to the business segment, a large, room-filling wall graphic was implemented in the entrance area, showing a historical photograph of roofers at work.

← Floor numbers in the staircase

↗ Detail overview and signpost
↘ Tea kitchen pictogram
↓ Pictograms

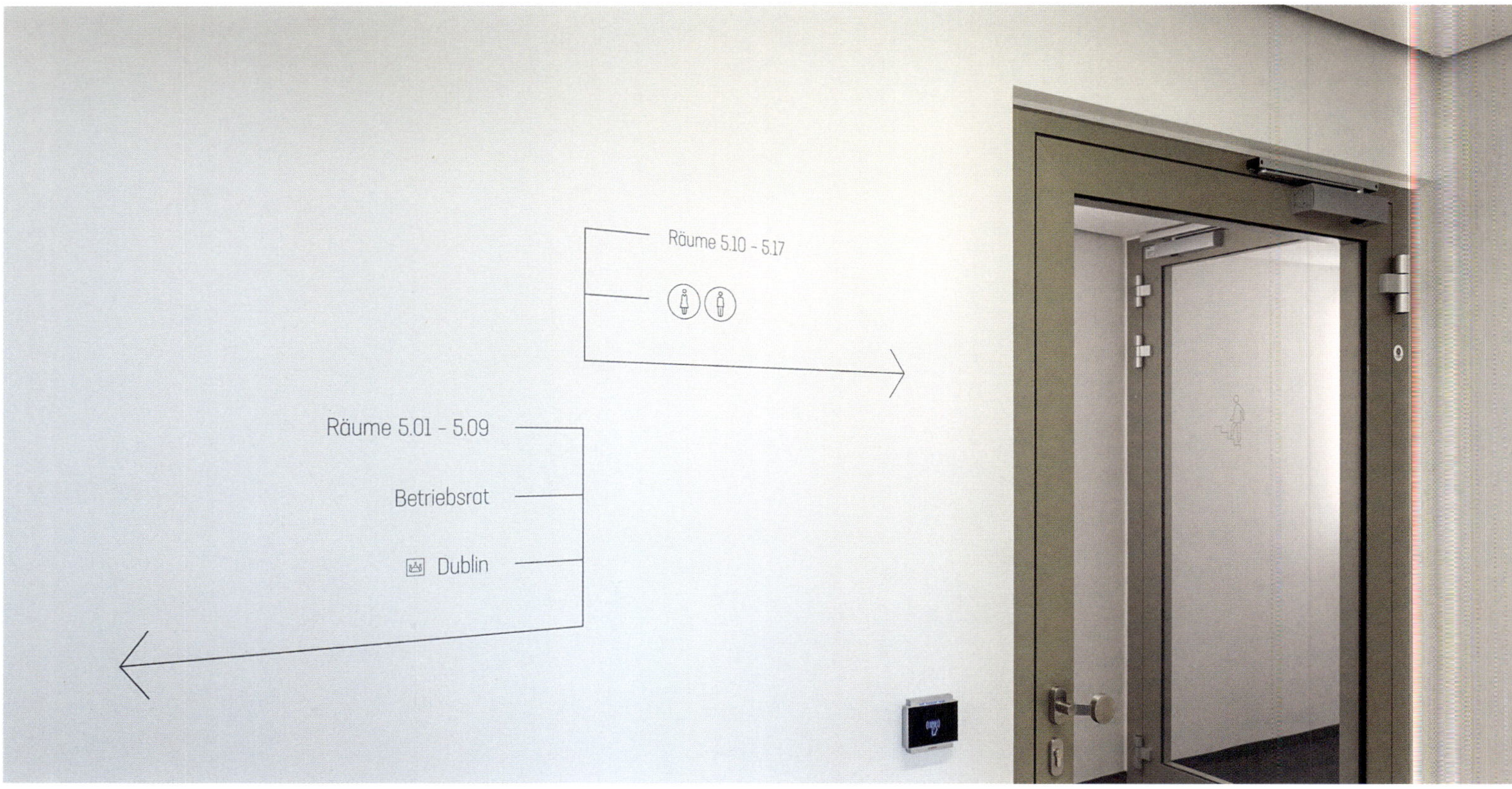

↑ Signpost
↓ Detail signpost and pictograms

→ Detail signpost and pictograms
↓ Overview, floor number and signpost

→→ Backlight effect
↘ Flat lettering contrasts spacious number on the fourth floor

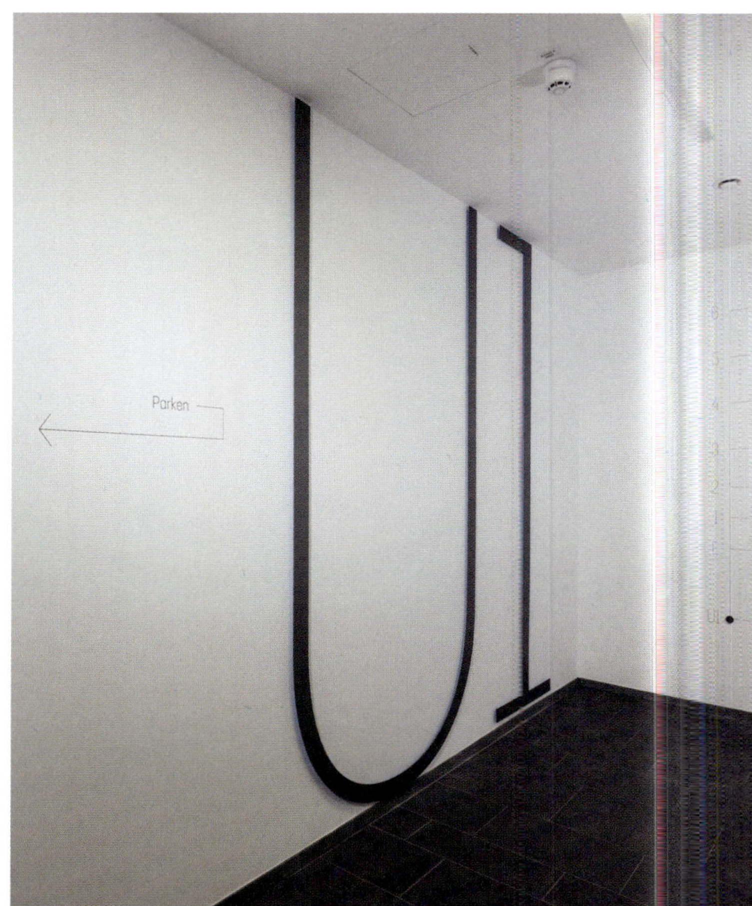

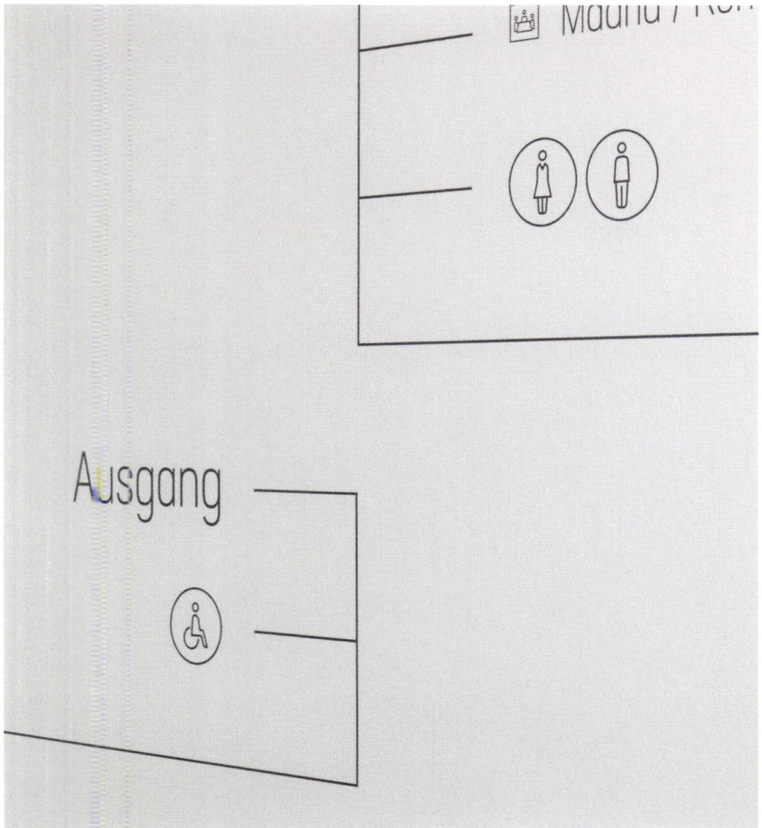
Ausgang

Parken

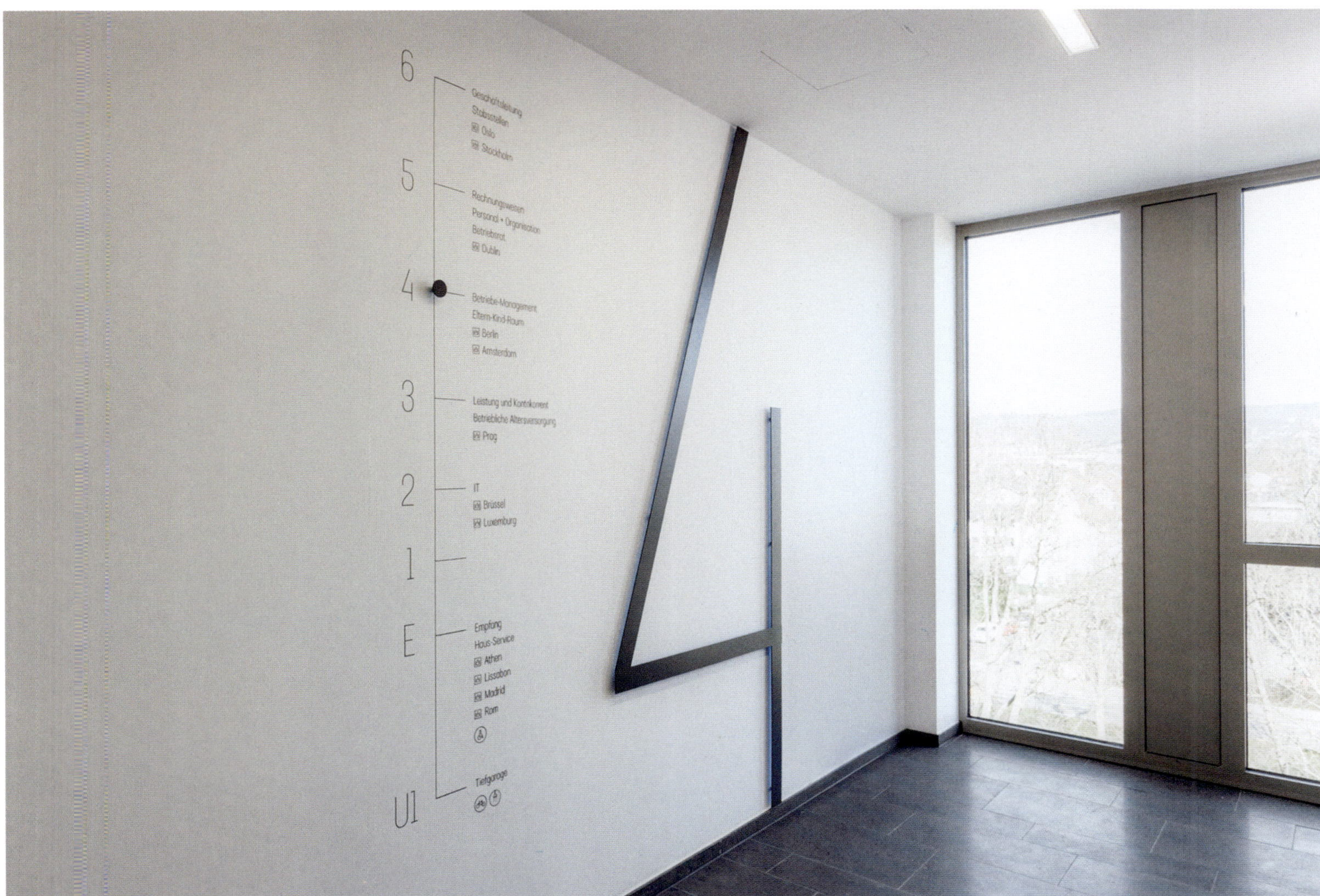
6
Geschäftsleitung
Stabsstellen
Oslo
Stockholm
5
Rechnungswesen
Personal + Organisation
Betriebsrat
Dublin
4
Betriebs-Management
Eltern-Kind-Raum
Berlin
Amsterdam
3
Leistung und Kontokorrent
Betriebliche Altersversorgung
Prag
2
IT
Brüssel
Luxemburg
1
E
Empfang
Haus-Service
Athen
Lissabon
Madrid
Rom
U1
Tiefgarage

Peckham Levels Wayfinding System

Designer Alexander Owen Architecture
Location London, United Kingdom
Client Make Shift
Completion 2018
Paint contractor Decorating Company UK
Function Work

Being themselves occupants of Peckham Levels, the architects were tasked by Make Shift with developing an internal wayfinding system for the building, as the start of an ongoing sequence of placemaking projects for the site. The design began by analyzing the building in both two and three dimensions, in order to understand the various entry/exit points as well as the internal ramp systems. The resulting wayfinding system and graphic form was born out of this analysis of the building's organization, as well as the way people move through it. The colors and graphic forms have been combined in an effort to help occupants and visitors navigate around this surprisingly simple, yet surprisingly disorientating building. One of the unexpected complexities in analyzing the building derived from how stairwells and lifts led to certain floors, while an internal ramp provided access to the others. It was this split-level nature of the building that needed to be represented in a simple graphic form in order to make the relatively confusing circulation routes more easily navigable. Colored light filters to suit each color code were installed so that the colors on the stairwell surfaces are themselves almost luminous. This means that as visitors move up and down the levels their eyes and visual perception of the space have to adapt to each of the different lighting conditions. This process of adaptation within the chromatic experience is an integral part of the wayfinding system, in that visitors are made to feel physically aware that they are transitioning to a new level within the building. Each of the final colors was chosen specifically to work in isolation and importantly in unison and ordered to enhance the clarity and experience of transitioning from level to level. The way in which visitor's visual and physical perception of each floor level adapts as they ascend and descend the stairwell, elevates Alexander Owen's system from a simple visitor journey into an immersive visitor experience.

← View from split-level 2
↙ Three-dimensional axonometric drawing of the stairwell

↑ View from blue level 3 entry

↑ View from split-level 2
↓ View from blue level 3 entry

↓ View from red level 1 entry

→ View from blue level 3 entry

PECKHAM LEVELS
The public levels can be found at the top of the stairs
CCTV in operation

start-up
besprechungsräume
123456

konsequent
Innovation
fördern

aws Headquarters Signage

Designer buero bauer Gesellschaft für Orientierung und Identität
Location Vienna, Austria
Client aws - Austria Wirtschaftsservice
Completion 2013
Interior designer Ingo Schumann
Typeface Helvetica Neue
Function Work

A new office building for the Austria Wirtschaftsservice, a federal development and financing bank for the promotion and financing of companies, required not only a new corporate design but a new spatial identity. First points of contact in the new building is the distinctively designed service desk in the entrance area. The rooms behind the area are for meetings and all three building levels are structured by the signage design. The corporate architecture of the furnishing of the kitchens, offices and meeting zones blend with the orientation system and are inviting, yet give the building a strong identity. It refers to the illustrative world of the corporate design, e.g. as a part of a widespread glass decoration made of sandblasted foil. The corporate color blue symbolizes the integrity of the institution.

↖ Interior signaling and impact protection
← Reception counter entrance area

↑ Corporate color blue and pictograms
← Pictograms

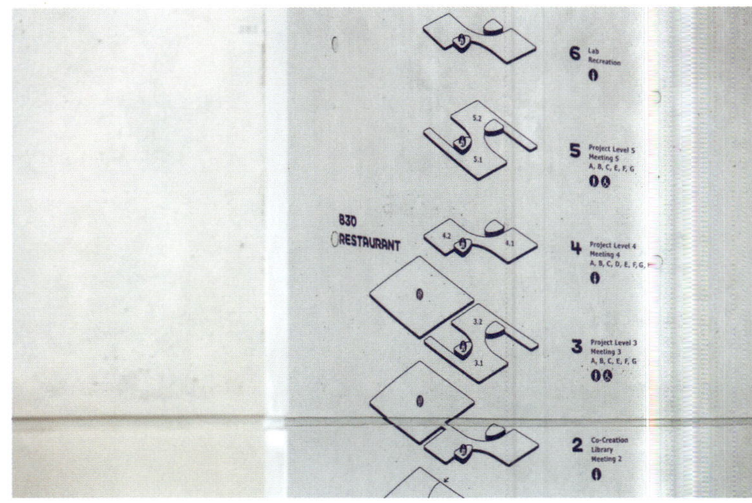

Merck – Innovation Center

↖ Signage, auditorium
↑↑ User interface via touch panel
↑ Floor plans, directly on the concrete core
↗ Directional arrow and floor number
→ Foyer

Designer Moniteurs Communication Design
Location Darmstadt, Germany
Client Merck KGaA
Completion 2018
Architect HENN
Typeface Verdana Pro, Merck Font
Function Work

The science and technology company Merck is expanding its Darmstadt location into its global headquarters. The historic industrial site is being transformed into a "Merck City": Modern infrastructure, a new Innovation Center and new modern production and office buildings create an innovative working environment for the more than 10,000 employees. The orientation concept, which was developed in a co-creating process with Merck and HENN, is comprehensive: Outdoor and indoor signage serve as strong brand elements on the Merck premises for orientation. Individual "types" each take on specific tasks: informing, pointing the way and marking locations. Merck introduced a new corporate brand identity in 2015 – colorful, with fascinating microbial and cell structures and a friendly visual language, the company communicates its strengths: openness, innovation, inventiveness, diversity. The stringent orientation concept contains a uniform wording and "Vibrant Highlight Elements", which not only depict but also create the color and structure of the new image. It is not a modular system, but an additive system with individual, concise "types".

Level

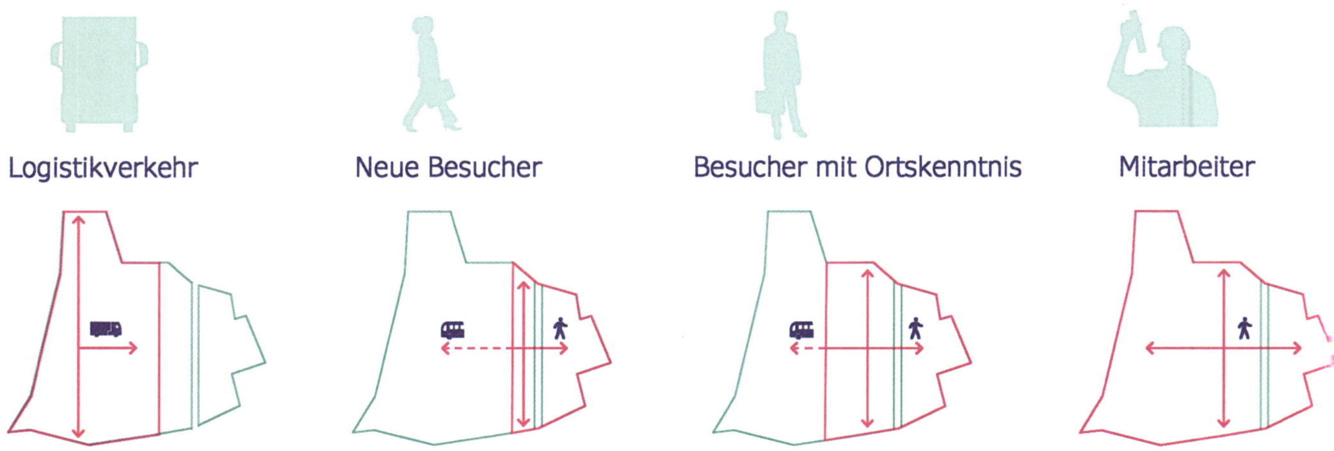

↑ Signage elements and pictograms

← Signage on glass

↓ Outdoor signage on the Merck premises

→ Subtle wayfinding in seating areas
↓ Seamless transition from branding and signage in the foyer of the research laboratory

C
‹AEF D›

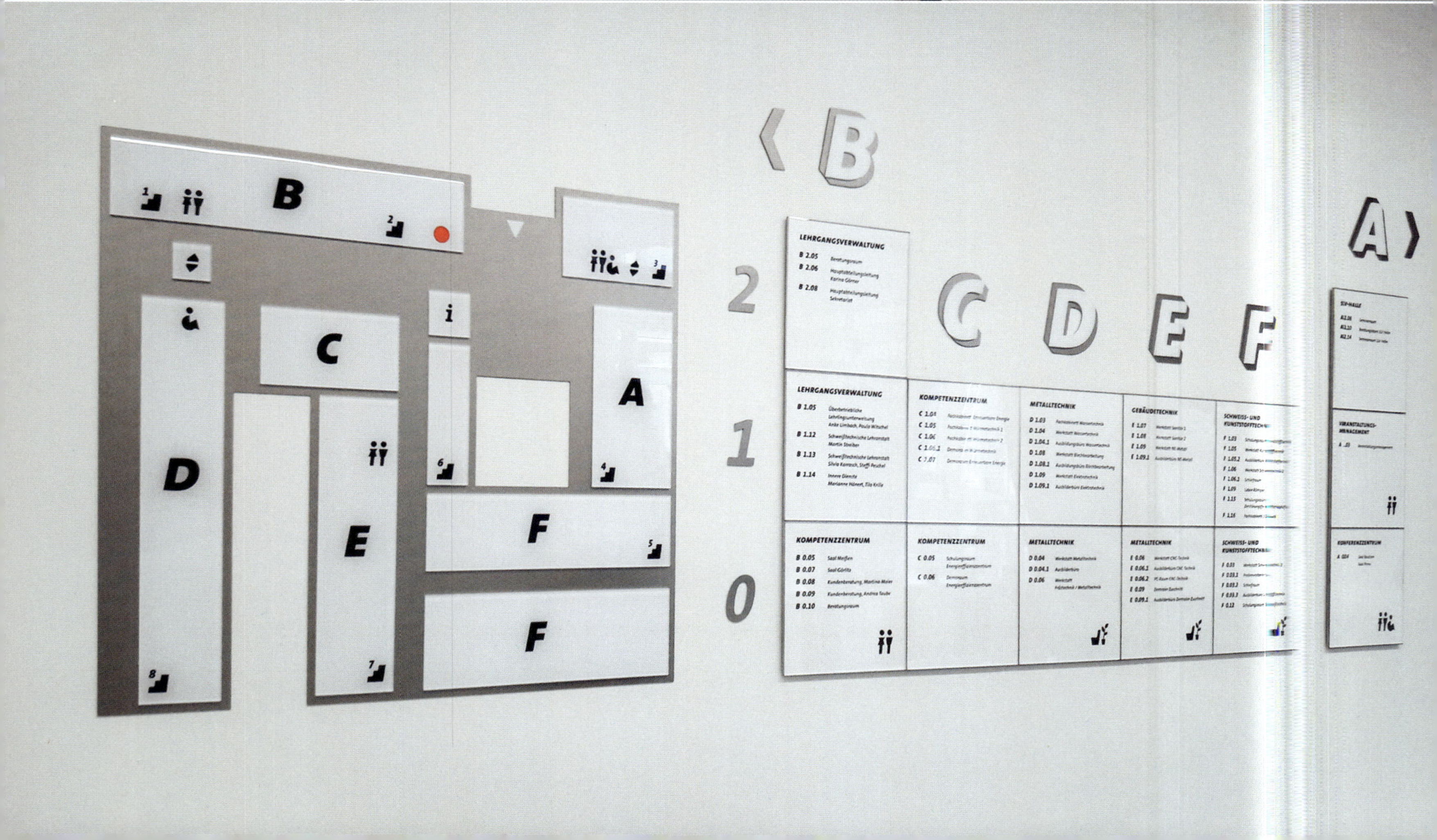
B
C
A
D
E
F
F
‹B
A›
2
1
0
C D E F
LEHRGANGSVERWALTUNG
KOMPETENZZENTRUM
METALLTECHNIK
GEBÄUDETECHNIK

Dresden Chamber of Trades and Crafts

Designer Form & Fokus
Location Dresden, Germany
Client Handwerkskammer Dresden
Completion 2019
Architect Architekturbüro Michael Auerbacher
Typeface TheSans
Function Education

With the construction of the new training center, the Chamber of Trades and Crafts achieved the centralization and modernization of its training facilities in Dresden. In the "Campus Bildungszentrum Handwerk Dresden", modern workshops in the fields of building services engineering, metal construction and welding technology, classrooms and training rooms close to the workshops as well as a conference area were created on approximately 7,300 square meters of floor space. The guidance system provides access to the existing buildings as well as to the interior and exterior of the new training center. It meets the requirements for a high-quality, low-maintenance and easily updated information and orientation system. The typology of information elements includes freestanding steles for area marking and signposting, parking space markings and building markings in the outdoor area as well as individual signposts, staircase identifiers, floor overviews and destination confirmations in the indoor area.

In addition, it represents not just the Campus but also the Chamber of Trades and Crafts and the numerous trades it stands for as an umbrella organization. Symbolizing the multitude of processing materials in the crafts, the individual information carriers are made of a combination of two different materials. The individually milled aluminum forms in combination with acrylic glass elements also refer to craftsmanship and skill; their inclined, italic alignment conveys dynamism and development.

← Destination confirmation, area identification, doorplate
↙ Orientation, building overview, floor plan

↑ Destination confirmation
← Signposts

Dresden Chamber of Trades and Crafts

← Orientation, building overview, floor plan, detail
→ Doorplate

←← Destination confirmation, area identification, doorplate
← Destination confirmation, close-up
→ Signposts, pictograms

24
THINK TANK
INTENSE WORKFLOW
EXPERIENCE

GfK Berlin

Designer IFUB*
Location Berlin, Germany
Client GfK SE
Completion 2016
Interior designer Vitra IDS and IFUB*
Function Work

For GfK SE, the new Berlin office was not only intended to concentrate the staff at the location, but also to become a pilot project for the start of a new office age. Vitra, an expert in new working environments, and IFUB*, a local cooperation partner, were therefore commissioned. The new, central office space was relocated to Berlin's Oberbaum City, formerly also known as Lampenstadt.
The open and versatile office space concept was tailored precisely to the work processes and wishes of the users. Conventional office cells were removed to achieve the desired open structures. The result are airy, bright rooms that revive the original spatial effect of the factory building and in which the most diverse possibilities for collaboration are now possible. Particular attention was paid to excellent room acoustics, which was achieved, among other things, by means of absorbers suspended in white structural steel grids. Built-in furniture made of birch with elaborate details provide order in a playful way.

↑ Open space office
↓ Handle detail and socket letters

↖ Room number
← Open space

↑ Common room and platform
← Common room and reception
↓ Grid ceiling

→ Large built-in cupboard
↓ Neon sign

Edelrid-Signaletik

Designer Studio SÜD-Visuelle Kommunikation
Location Isny im Allgäu, Germany
Client Edelrid GmbH
Completion 2019
Typeface Sektor E (self-constructed), Corporate S (corporate font Edelrid, Kurt Weidemann)
Function Work

For Edelrid's new office building – the company produces climbing equipment – Studio SÜD-Visuelle Kommunikation has developed a guidance system and wall displays in which the three-dimensional font Sektor E serves as the main element. The essence of the mountain is inherent in the font: The letters are defined by the sharp ridge. They are constructed in a linear way and are designed for two-dimensional applications as well as for the production of three-dimensional signs. They are used for the marking of eleven conference rooms, which were given poetic imaginative names referring to mountains such as "Euphorie Eck", "Jubeljoch" or "Stille Kuppe". Set vertically, they resemble the direction of movement while climbing. The wooden letters are also used in striking floor overviews: A graphic of the "Hochgrat" covers concrete walls in the foyer and staircase. A mounted climbing rope marks the route from the valley to the summit – ergo along various stations from the registration desk on the ground floor to the management on the second floor.

← Detail of the three-dimensional letters

↑ Three-dimensional letters
← Sektor E, two-dimensional

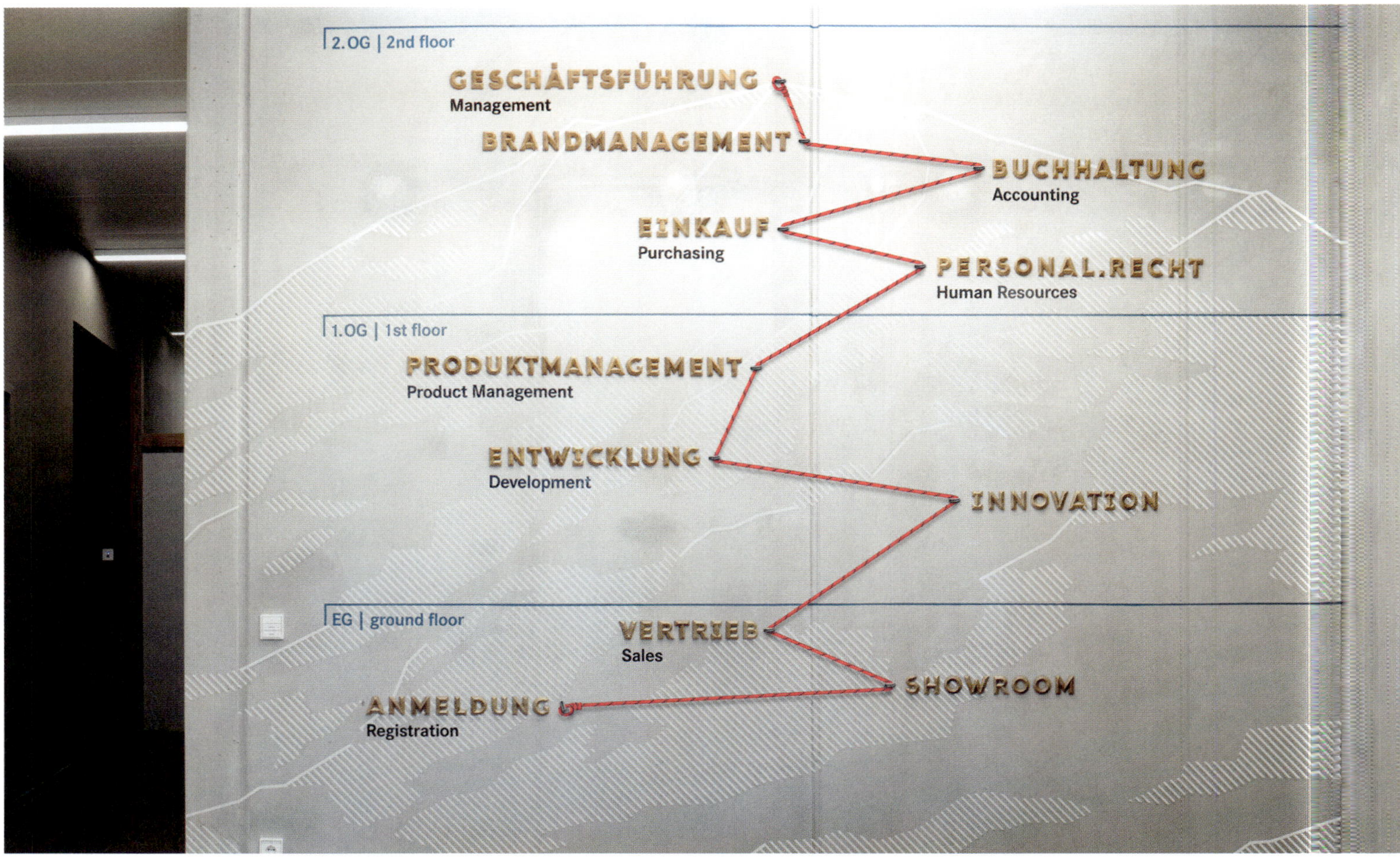

↑ Floor overview in the foyer
← Lettering of the conference rooms
↓ Sektor E, three-dimensional

→ Detail of the three-dimensional letters
↓ Lettering of the conference rooms, samples
↘ Lettering of the conference room "Aussichtsfelsen"

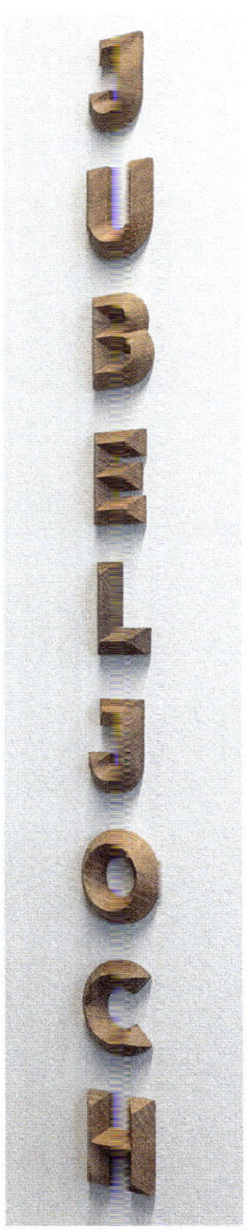

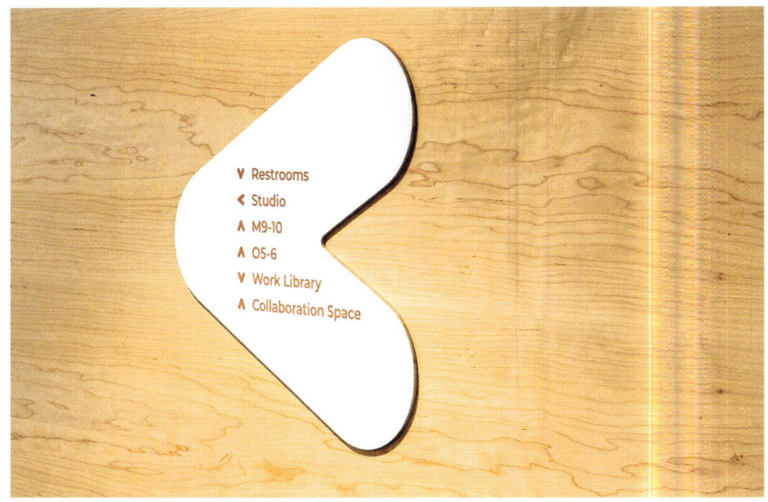

SAGE Publications

↖ Pictogram on oval panel Library
↑↑ Arches marking a hallway
↑ Simplified arrows for quick directional wayfinding
↗ Artful mix of open and private workspaces
→ Neon entry sign

<u>Designer</u> Blitz
<u>Location</u> Thousand Oaks, CA, USA
<u>Client</u> SAGE Publications
<u>Completion</u> 2019
<u>Typeface</u> Montserrat (SemiBold)
<u>Function</u> Work

For the retrofit of the 50,000-square-foot location (4,645 square meters), the Los Angeles office of Blitz conceived an interior that reflects SAGE Publications' mission, which is based on the belief that engaged scholarship lies at the heart of any healthy society and that education is intrinsically valuable.

Blitz's graphics department created a robust wayfinding signage package (in multiple locations across the floorplan), custom room signage, glazing graphics identifying private rooms, and a neon entry sign of SAGE Publications' logo.

Wall signs are made from sealed oak to match other material finishes in the project, and alternate between white graphics on oak and an oak-like color on white, depending on their placement. Simplified arrows with Montserrat (SemiBold) typeface for quick directional wayfinding correspond to architectural elements, such as arches and rounded volumes. Room names on oval panels are denoted by pictograms to maintain consistency in the layout and avoid graphic challenges presented by names of varying lengths. As well, since SAGE Publications is an international company, Blitz wanted to use a visual vocabulary that easily communicates to all audiences, regardless of language.

SAGE
Publishing

Library
2
1
Medical
Centre
0
Exit
Bicycle
Parking
-1
Changing
Rooms

ECB – Signage and Information System

<u>Designer</u> unit-design
<u>Location</u> Frankfurt am Main, Germany
<u>Client</u> European Central Bank
<u>Completion</u> 2016
<u>Architect</u> Coop Himmelb(l)au
<u>Typeface</u> StradaPro
<u>Function</u> Administration

The European Central Bank (ECB) is an institution, not a typical bank with its own brand strategy. The spectacular building of Coop Himmelb(l)au is the brand. In its successful combination with the historic wholesale market hall (Martin Elsaesser, 1928) it has changed Frankfurt's cityscape forever from all views. The signage and orientation system connects the generously interwoven spatial structures and different materials by means of background-colored, seemingly floating markings. The functional task of intuitively guiding employees and, above all, visitors to the campus-like ensemble with its diverse facilities for meetings and conferences through the building is supplemented by signage system elements that appear to be independent and present even from a distance. Font and pictograms were developed especially for the different use of elements digitally cut. The system, which consists of more than 8,000 individual positions, harmonizes with both, the modern office building and the historic monument.

← Floor overview in the former wholesale market hall
↓ Marking of the central lift group
→ Detail directional stele
↘ Marking with remote effect

abcdefghijklmn
opqrtsuvwxyz
ABCDEFGHIJKLMN
OPQRSTUVWXYZ
1234567890

abcdeéfghijklm
nopqrtsuvwxyz
ABCDEFGHIJKLM
NOPQRSTUVWXYZ
1234567890 _

abcdefghijklmn
opqrtsuvwxyz
ABCDEFGHIJKLMN
OPQRSTUVWXYZ
1234567890

_abcdeéfghijklm
nopqrtsuvwxyz_
_ABCDEFGHIJKLM
NOPQRSTUVWXYZ_
1234567890 ___

↑ StradaPro and derived typography
↓ Digital and analogue signage to meeting rooms

↓ Guide to special destinations

↑ Pictograms
↗ Sign on historical facade
→ Guide conference area
→→ Outdoor pylon

Library

EUROPEAN CENTRAL BANK
EUROSYSTEM
European Central Bank
Sonnemannstrasse 20
60314 Frankfurt am Main
Besucherparkplatz
Visitor Car Park
Anlieferung

Harper's

Hearst Tower

Designer C&G Partners
Location New York, USA
Client Hearst Corporation
Completion 2006
Architect Foster + Partners, Architects
Executive architect Adamson Associates
Interior designer Gensler
Typeface Garamond 3 Italic, News Gothic Regular
Function Work

The 1928 art deco building that was the home of the Hearst Corporation in Manhattan has been reinvented. Foster + Partners, Architects have inserted a 44-story steel and glass tower inside of the six-story cast stone structure. The landmark façade is now a single, 21-meter-high, sky-lit atrium space.
The challenge of the sign program was to design a system that would integrate into both the historic façade as well as the minimalist modern tower. The solution is a system of signs whose keynote is an array of freestanding "totems" made out of glass and stainless steel that serve many important functions. In addition to identification and directional information, the totems house the lobby's security cameras and the call buttons for a sophisticated Miconic elevator system.

← Looking into offices from elevator lobby
↙ Internally illuminated bronze entrance signs
↑ Sign totem keypad in use

The rest of the sign program key off the totem design with typefaces carefully chosen to relate to the corporate identity of the Hearst organization.
In addition to the public spaces, the sign system extends into the office tower. The office signage takes advantage of wealth of graphic identity inherent in the media organizations that are part of the Hearst family.

Aimer Lingerie Factory Complex

↖↖ Handrail signage detail
↖ Signage in lobby area
↑ Signage stele at entrance of inner landscape
↗ Handrail signage at inner landscape
→ Metal façade and gray signage stele

<u>Designer</u> Crossboundaries, Beijing
<u>Location</u> Beijing, China
<u>Client</u> Beijing Aimer Lingerie Co., Ltd.
<u>Completion</u> 2014
<u>Architect</u> Crossboundaries, Beijing
<u>Collaborators architecture</u> BIAD International Studio & BIAD TSH International Studio
<u>Function</u> Work

Aimer Lingerie Factory Center is more than a factory. Besides the production line for mainly lingerie and its distribution center, the building complex contains research and development offices, a conference center, a lobby with an adjacent shop and a museum.
The signage and wayfinding system tie these diverse functions together to achieve a consistent image, which reflects the essence of lingerie. The reduced color palette for the signage follows the architecture. Only in the office area red is introduced as a secondary color. The freestanding gray metal steles outside the complex act in coherence with the metal façade, the slightly tilted planes display white letters.
On other surface materials like stone or glass, occurring inside the building and on the open outside deck, the application is reversed with dark, mostly independent letters. To distinguish different functional areas, capital letters are introduced with a shaded line to appear three-dimensional and prominent.
Functional icons mainly used in the office areas are applying the figure ground principle allowing for a certain playfulness.

A4 生产区
Production
A5 物流区
Distribution
研发办公区
R&D Office
A3

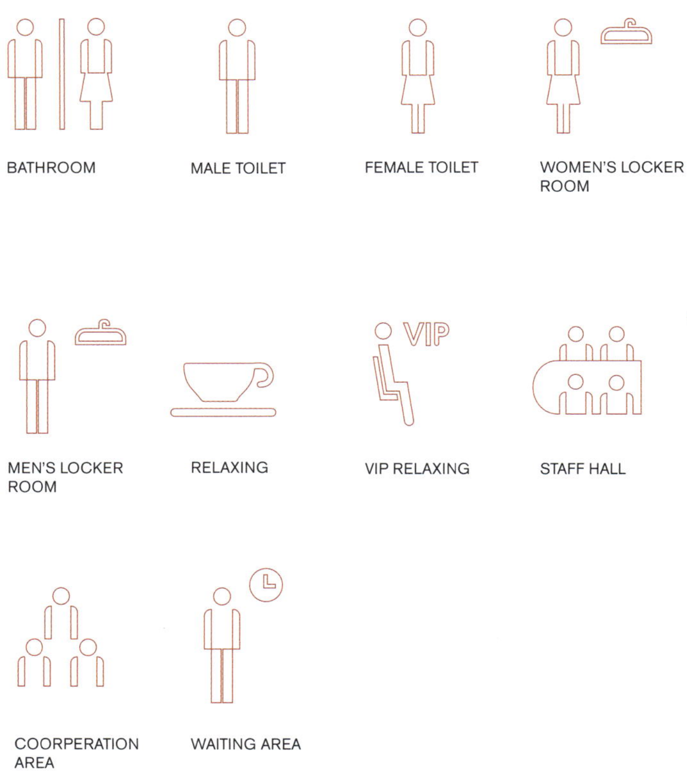

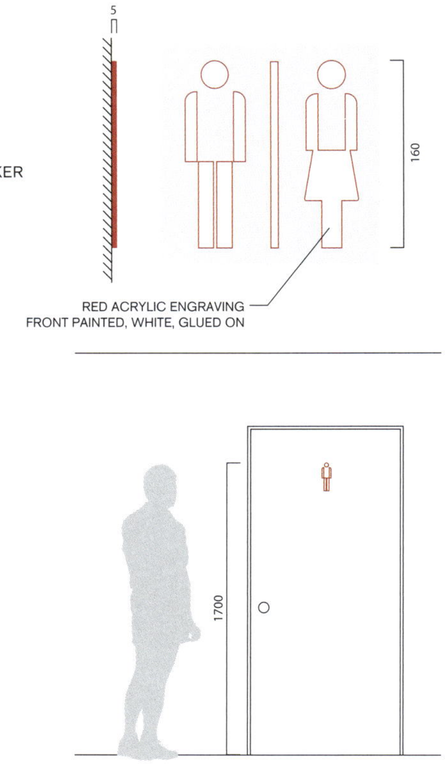

↑ Signage for office area
↓ Freestanding stele

→ Signage stele at entrance of factory complex

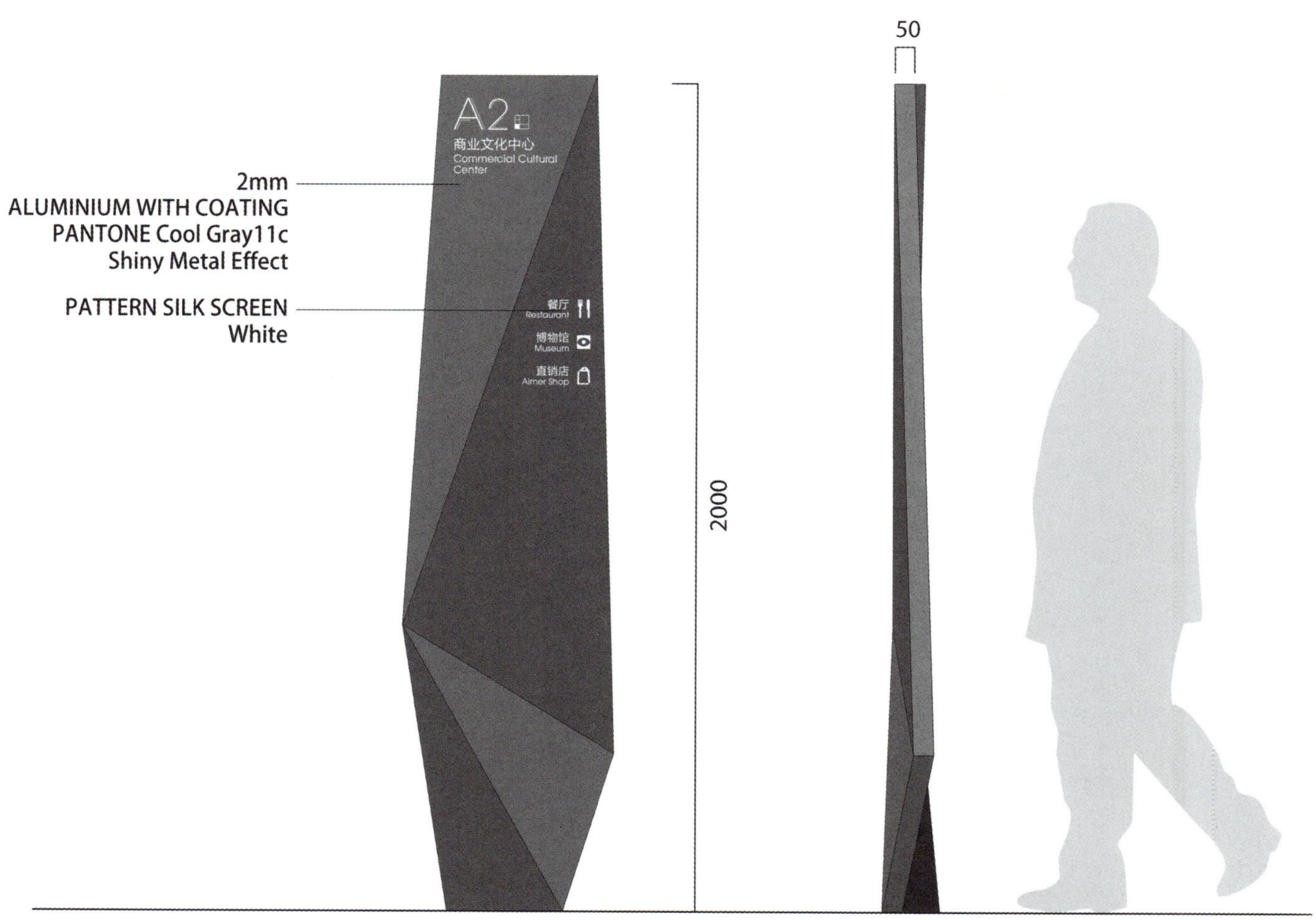

↑
A1
大堂
Lobby
A3
研发办公区
R&D Office
Center

SAAL 2–3
RAUM 101–252
WOLKE BLAU
EBENE 2
KONFERENZRAUM 202–252
WOLKE BLAU
EBENE 1
SAAL 2–3
KONFERENZRAUM 101–107
EBENE 0
SAAL 1
SERVICEBEREICHE
EBENE -1
PARKEBENE 1
KASSENAUTOMAT
EBENE -2
PARKEBENE 2

Stuttgart Region Chamber of Commerce and Industry, Signage System

Designer büro uebele visuelle kommunikation
Location Stuttgart, Germany
Client Stuttgart Region Chamber of Commerce and Industry
Completion 2014
Architect Wulf Architekten
Typeface FF DIN
Function Work

Where to, and where next? Visitors to the new Stuttgart Region Chamber of Commerce and Industry building are welcomed and guided to their destination by cheerful bands of color. Even if their route leads up a hidden staircase, visitors can tell at once where they are heading: from the two-story foyer they can already see the colorful signs on the floor above. Clear information is presented on multi-colored wallpaper – the layered stripes blending in naturally with the architecture. At each new wayfinding point the pattern of bright colors is configured differently, reflecting and communicating the diversity of the Stuttgart Region.

← Downstairs foyer

↑ View from upper level
↓ Garage

↑ Foyer entrance
↓ Office corridor with glass wall

↗ Foyer screens
→ Office corridor
→→ Staircase

KONFERENZ
RAUM
230
KONFERENZRAUM 232–23
WC DAMEN
KONFERENZRAUM 202–228
AUFZUG
TREPPENHAUS

EBENE
2
KONFERENZRAUM 202–252
WOLKE BLAU

wejście
entrance

Nowy Targ

Designer Kolektyf
Location Wroc□aw, Poland
Client Skanska
Completion 2019
Typeface Dedicated
Function Work

Kolektyf was responsible for designing the building signage for the commercial and office facility Nowy Targ on Pl. Nowy Targ 28, 50-438 in Wrocław, ordered by Macków Pracowania Projektowa design studio. The project is located in the center of Wrocław. The building stands out with its pea gravel concrete finish, and a façade with a dominating characteristic rhythm. A large part of the interior common area is finished with raw concrete. The building's architecture provided the inspiration to limit the means of expression and apply minimalism in the design. Large, stylish typography and solid, decisive cuts in terms of graphics were chosen to enhance the architecture.

↖ Signage with the indication of the communication lines
← Entire wall signage of garage level

↑ Signs indicating restrooms
← Pictograms

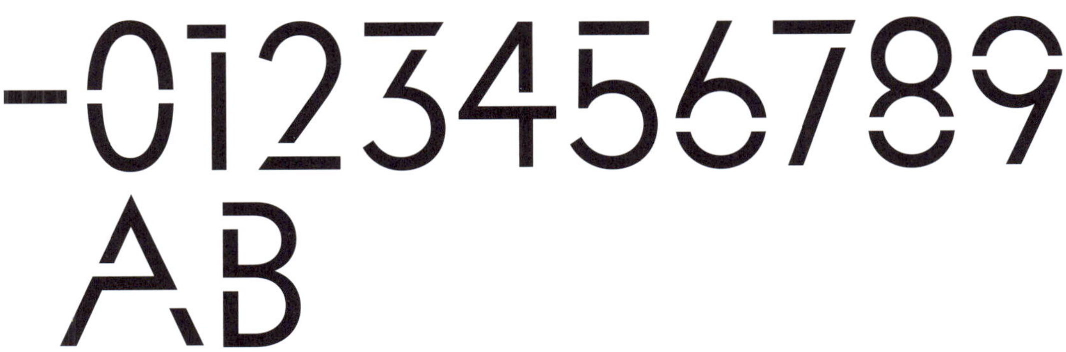

↑ Big, contrasting directional signage on concrete
↓ Wi-Fi and garage signage

↓ Wall mark of the floor number in the staircase

→ Contrast marking the exit from the garage level to the elevator

wejście
entrance
iB

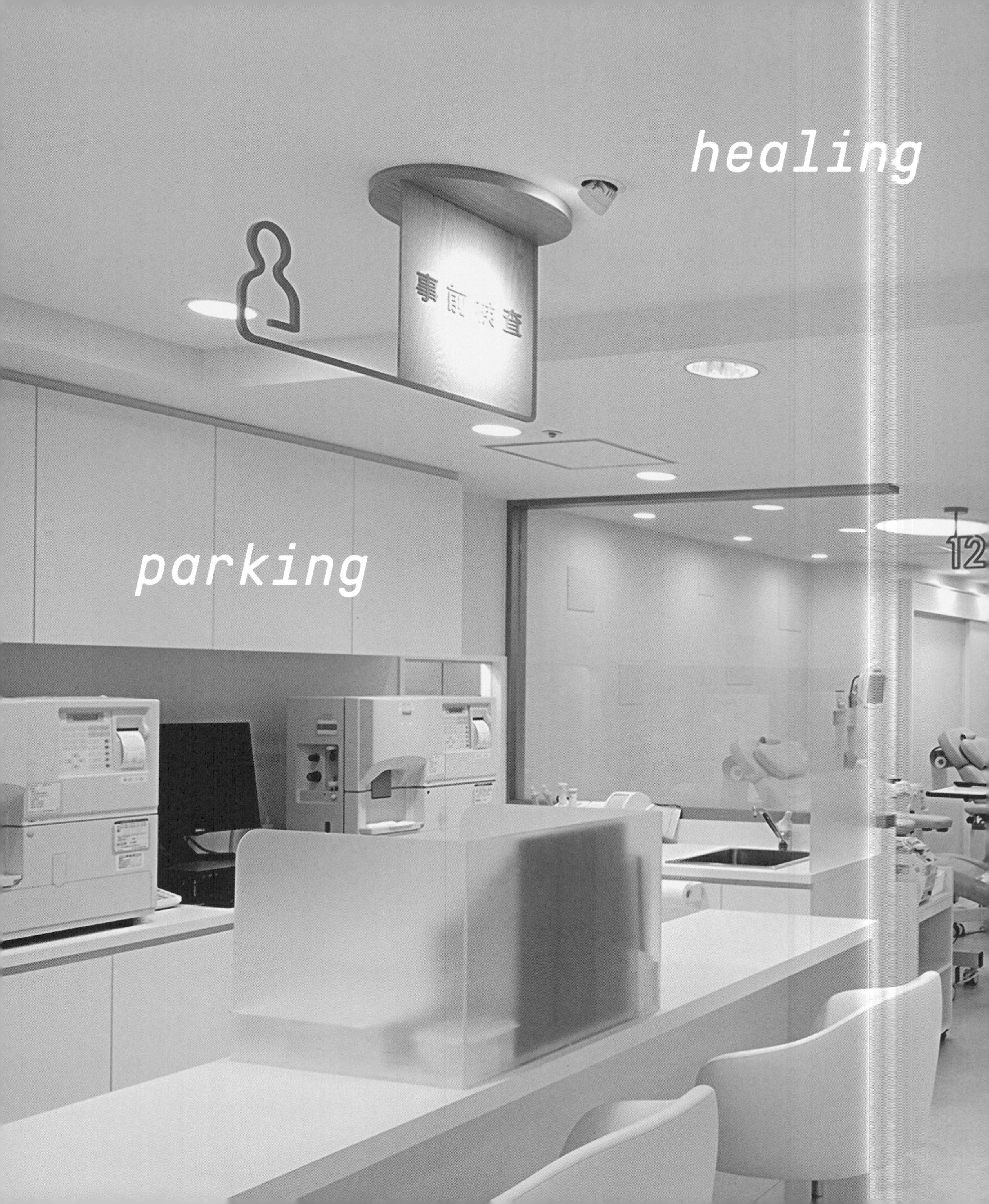
healing
parking

fast wayfinding

traveling

C
D
E
F

Children's Hospital Colorado

Designer ArtHouse Design
Location Aurora, CO, USA
Client Children's Hospital Colorado
Completion 2011
Typeface Interstate
Function Public

One of the top 10 children's hospitals in the United States, Children's Hospital Colorado is a state-of-the-art healthcare complex at Aurora's Anschutz Medical Campus. Children's Hospital Colorado is also home to Colorado's only level one pediatric trauma center and is one of only eight stand-alone pediatric research centers in the United States.
With more than 4,000 interior and exterior wayfinding elements, environmental graphics and donor signage features, this impressive undertaking emphasizes the level of care that patients receive here on a daily basis. ArtHouse developed an iconic system of graphics that incorporates a playful color palette, exciting points of discovery and inspiring interactive features to complement the spirit and vitality of Children's Hospital Colorado.

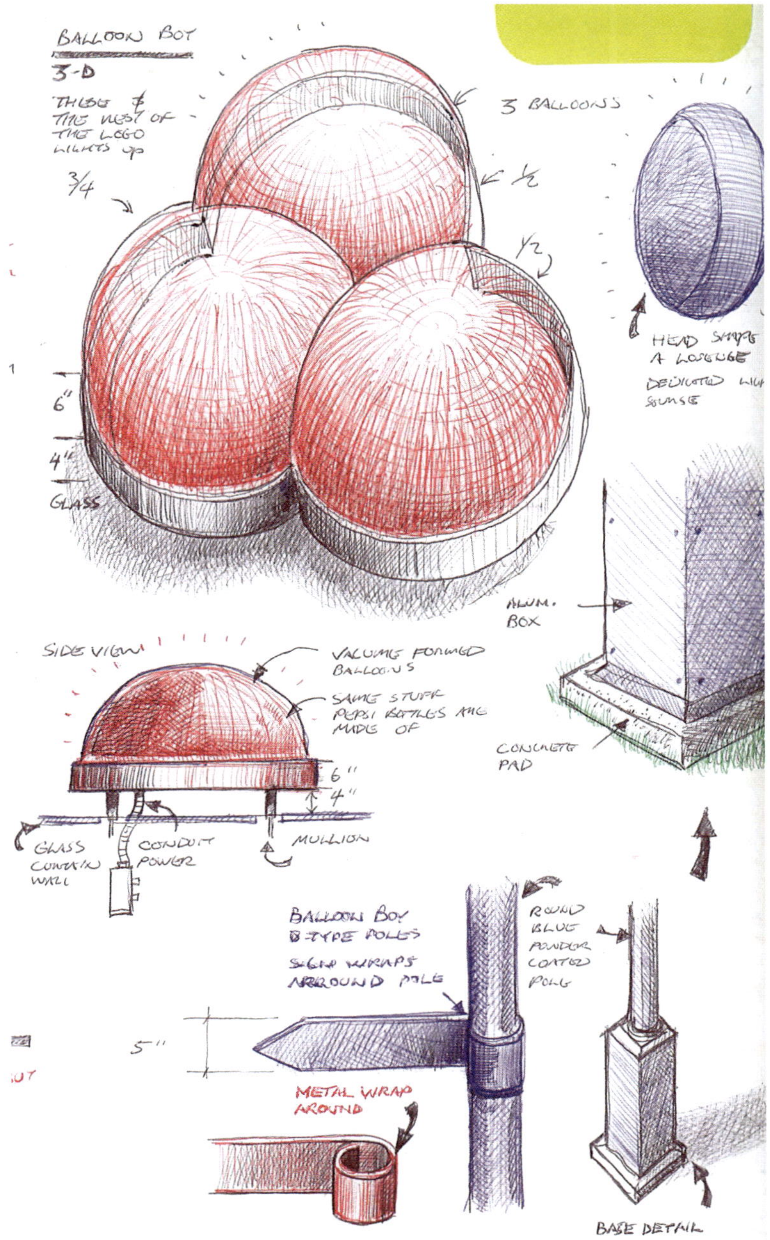

↖ Exterior signage featuring the hospital's logo as an oversized sculpture
← Outpatient rooms are identified by letter, color and animal
→ Concept sketch of the 3D logo for exterior signage
↓ Level icons for the main campus building

↑ Theming graphics
← Exterior signage and building mounted signage

↓ Concept sketch of the 3D logo for exterior signage

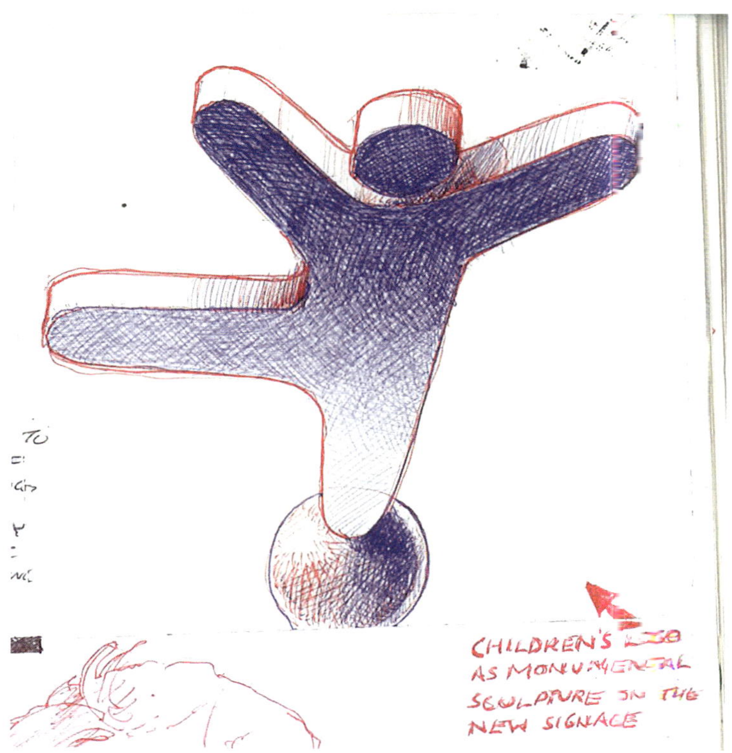

→ Check-in area for the surgery center
↓ Third floor interior wayfinding sign color-coded to match the floor color

UP TO 1 HOUR
26.19
UP TO 2 HOURS 37.17
UP TO 10 HOURS 41.39
UP TO 24 HOURS 49.00
SUV'S O'SIZE ADD'L 9.29
MONTHLY RATE 608.24
MAIN FLOOR 692.71
VANS O'SIZE ADD'L 84.48
18.375%
PARKING TAX EXTRA
AMPCO
SYSTEM PARKING
13-17 EAST 54TH ST.
LICENSE NO
1288781
CAPACITY 225
OPEN
24 HOURS
7 DAYS A WEEK
THE DEPARTMENT OF CONSUMER AFFAIRS OF THE CITY OF NEW YORK HAS ISSUED THE FOLLOWING
LICENSE TO THIS BUSINESS:
LICENSEE: AMPCO SYSTEM PARKING
LICENSE NO
1288781
ATTENTION MANHATTAN RESIDENTS:
BE ELIGIBLE FOR AN EXEMPTION FROM THE 8% PARKING TAX
CONTACT: NYC DEPARTMENT OF FINANCE PARKING TAX
NOTICE
VEHICLE BY FIRE, THEFT OR EXPLOSION LIMITED TO $25,000
UNLESS
ADDITIONAL FEE PAID WHEN VEHICLE FIRST PARKED
AND RECEIPT ISSUED FOR SAME.
ATTENDANT PARK
WAIT FOR PARKING TICKET. READ YOUR PARKING TICKET.
LEAVE IGNITION KEY ONLY.
ONLY ATTENDANTS WILL PARK AND DELIVER CARS.
CARS MUST BE LEFT WITH ATTENDANT.
NOT RESPONSIBLE FOR ANY ARTICLES LEFT IN CAR.
UNAUTHORIZED VEHICLES
WILL BE TOWED AWAY AT OWNER'S EXPENSE.
CHECK CLOSING HOURS.
MONTHLY ACCOUNTS MUST BE
PAID ON THE 1ST
OF EACH MONTH
OR DAILY RATES WILL BE CHARGED.
CARS
SUBJECT TO BEING HELD AFTER THE 5TH.
CARS SUBJECT TO ROOF PARKING WHEN APPROPRIATE.
CLAIMS
FOR DAMAGES WILL
NOT BE ACCEPTED
UNLESS
VEHICLE IS CHECKED
UPON ENTERING AND
LEAVING GARAGE
WE ARE NOT RESPONSIBLE
FOR REMOVABLE
RADIOS, STEREO
EQUIPMENT, RADAR

CHECKOUT
WAITING AREA
ALL MAJOR CREDIT CARDS ACCEPTED

Parking at 13–17 East 54th Street

Designer Pentagram
Location New York City, NY, USA
Client Cohen Bros. Realty
Completion 2010
Typeface Verlag
Function Traffic

Pentagram has designed graphics for a Midtown Manhattan garage that make sure drivers never forget where their car is. Owned by Cohen Bros. Realty and managed by Ampco System Parking, the seven-story garage is located at 13–17 East 54th Street, between Fifth and Madison Avenues and adjacent to an office building at 3 East 54th Street, also owned by Cohen. The owners planned to upgrade the garage and install a new program of environmental graphics. City zoning required more traditional signage on the façade, which has been rendered in elegant neon. The interior signage acts as a kind of backseat driver as one moves through the garage. Set in Verlag, the typographic pileup includes instructions for drivers: "Slow and steady wins the race", "Do not stop here, Continue", and so forth as well as supergraphics identifying parking levels and elevators.

↖ Wall signs and road arrows
← Waiting area

↑ Neon signage installed on the exterior of the garage
← Road arrows and garage numbers

Kawagoe – Blood Donation Room

↖ Kids room signage
↑↑ Drink corner signage
↑ Restroom sign
→ Number signs at blood donation booths
↓ Blood donation room

Designer 6D-K
Location Kawagoe, Japan
Client Japanese Red Cross Society
Completion 2011
Interior designer AIM Create Co.
Typeface Morisawa's Shingo / Swiss 721 BT / DIN
Function Health

This blood donation room is located in front of the station of Kawagoe, Saitama Prefecture. The signage is easy to understand, and aims at familiarity. The signs are mounted in different ways on each location, depending on the configuration with an one-stroke line of red. The numbers at the donor places are designed similar to unify the place. The one-stroke line in red represents the blood of the blood donation center and the connection between people through blood donation.

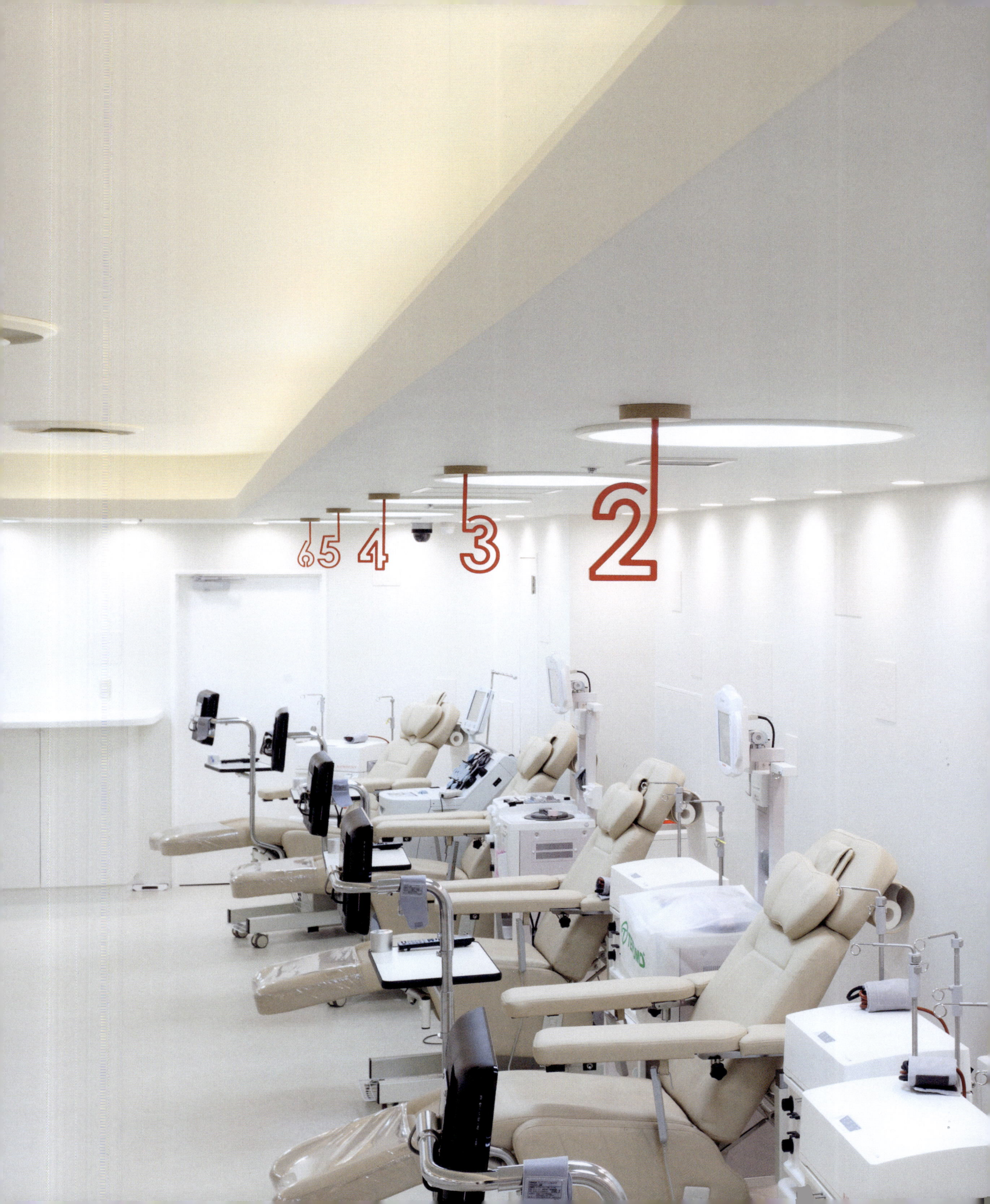
6
5
4
3
2

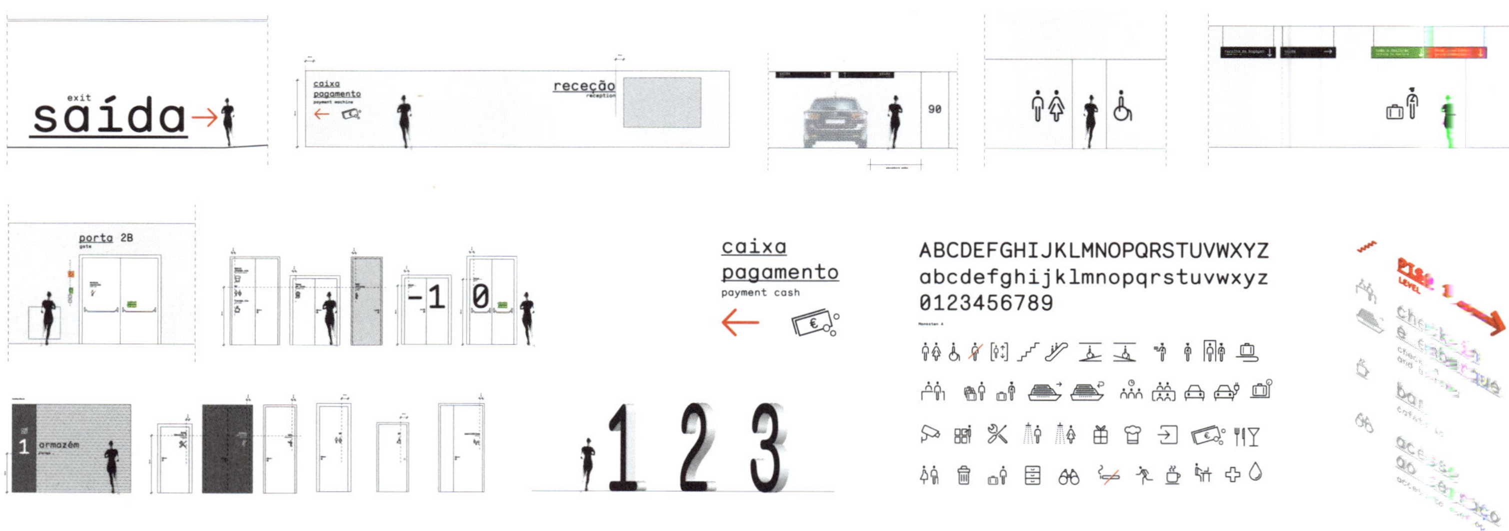

Lisbon Cruise Terminal

↖↖ Gate 03
↑ Pictograms, signs and typeface

↗↗ General directory
→ Exterior

Designer P-06 Atelier
Creative director Nuno Gusmão
Collaboration Mário Videira, Giuseppe Greco, Frederico Gonçalves
Location Lisbon, Portugal
Client Lisbon Cruise Port
Completion 2018
Architect JLCG Arquitectos
Typeface Monosten Regular
Function Traffic

The wayfinding system for the Lisbon Cruise Terminal was designed to be effective in delivering a clear, clean and accurate orientation, with a minimal design approach suited for the space and for this kind of equipment (similar to an airport but with a much smaller scale).
The graphic language itself aims to have a "friendly feel" to balance the modern sharp-angled architecture style of the building. Monosten Regular was the chosen typeface (a rounded monospaced typeface) because of its "smoothness", simple lines, and overall good legibility. To match the rounded typeface, a complete bespoke pictogram set was designed aiming to share the same graphic DNA of Monosten.
The color code of the signage system is mainly black and white with some notes of red alongside. The signage system has different scales suited to the needs of each specific moment of the passenger's route inside the Cruise Terminal, such as the oversized boarding gates' numbers, the big toilets pictograms, or entrance signs to be seen from distance, versus the directional signage and door signage designed to be effective within a close range.

entrada
entrance
entrega
de bagagem
luggage drop off
acesso
pisos -1.1.2
access to
levels -1.1.2

Caritas Daycare Center

<u>Designer</u> buero bauer Gesellschaft für Orientierung und Identität
<u>Location</u> Vienna, Austria
<u>Client</u> Caritas
<u>Completion</u> 2014
<u>Interior designer</u> Josh Reingruber
<u>Typeface</u> Helvetica
<u>Function</u> Hospitality

The first part of the newly opened Caritas Daycare Center close to the central railway station of Vienna offers homeless and people in need of help and care a place to stay during the day and support in their daily life tasks. To help them feel comfortable and oriented, a simple yet effective information system was integrated into bright and friendly rooms.
Raw and yellow varnished wooden panels were used to build furnishings and information carriers. They blend with the architecture yet stand out through their color. The pictogram-based visual language considers that the clients of the daycare center often have a varying language background. Warm and intense yellow in combination with the wooden structures support the well-being and sense of security at this hideaway for the outsiders of our society.

↖ Reception counter entrance area
← Directly printed pictograms on wooden surface

↑ Façade lettering
← Pictograms

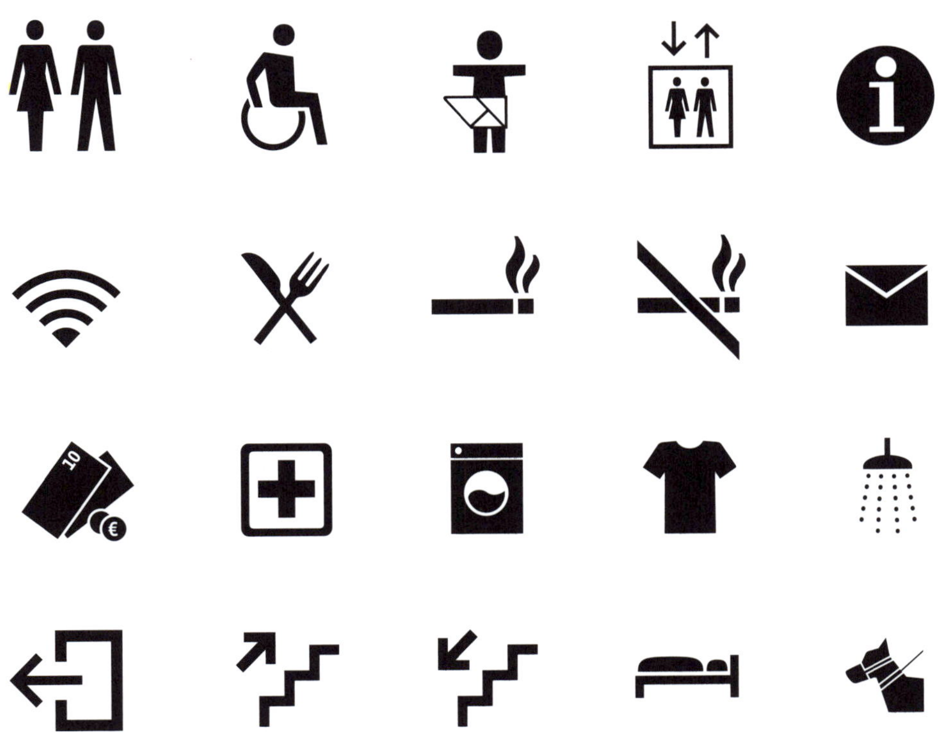

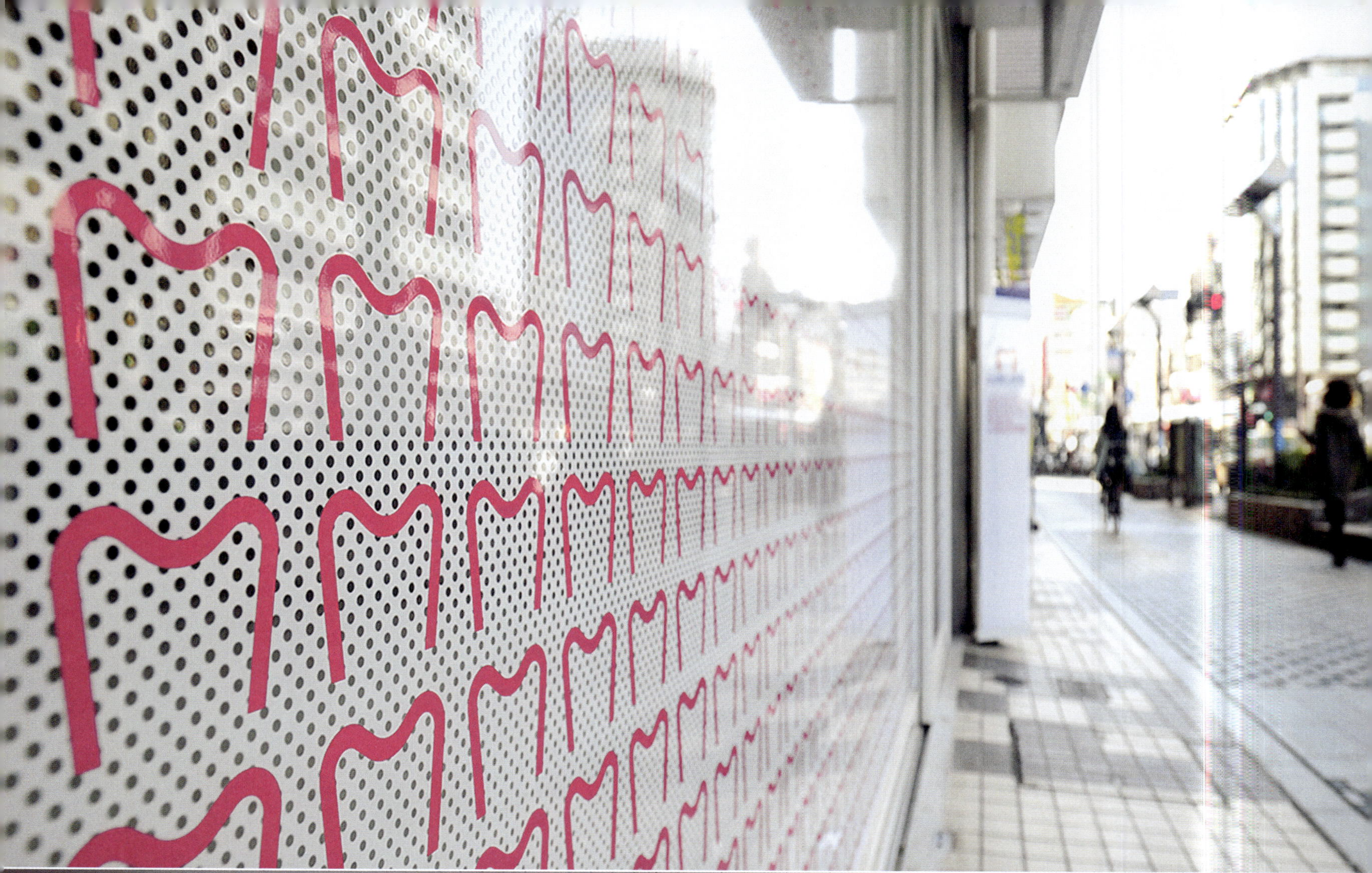

みなみ歯科・矯正歯科
MINAMI ORAL HEALTH CLINIC
Bigoff
5714-1785
地店圧倒価格
会社実印
角印
実印
銀行印
はん激安名刺
指定自立支援医療機関

Minami Oral Health Clinic

Designer TERADADESIGN ARCHITECTS
Location Tokyo, Japan
Client Minami Oral Health Clinic
Completion 2015
Function Health

For the renovation of this dental clinic, the client requested the creation of a new set of values to encompass the entire environment, consistent with the guiding principle of the clinic, which is "preventative dental care". Perceiving the concept of "preventative dental care" as the maintenance and improvement of "beautiful teeth", TERADADESIGN ARCHITECTS created a new symbol for the clinic, and endeavored to express the clinic's principles by utilizing this symbol throughout the entire space as an environmental graphic, from the façade to the interiors. The pink symbol that looks like an "M" is similar to the pictogram of a beautiful tooth. Many of these geometrically shaped lines line up neatly as a pattern. The ceilings, painted in pink to evoke the oral color of a healthy mouth, lead from the entrance to the treatment rooms. The treatment room symbols and pictograms placed symmetrically on both the ceiling and floor provide a rhythmic flow to the corridors, and make the space look deeper. In order to avoid confusion of the treatment room symbols with the tooth numbering system, they were designated with Japanese katana characters.

↖ Exterior view with close-up of the window front
← Exterior view
↓ The "M" symbol on the window front, inside

↑ Corridor with symbols on floor and ceiling
↓ Logo and graphic

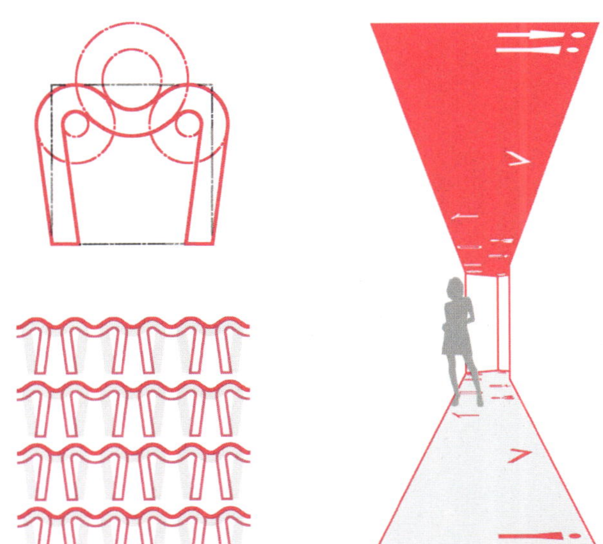

5
4
3

Queensland Children's Hospital

Designer Dotdash
Location Brisbane, Australia
Client Queensland Government Queensland Health
Completion 2015
Architect Conrad Gargett Lyons Architects
Typeface Helvetica Neue 55 Roman / 75 Bold
Function Health

Through a series of workshops, the team of Dotdash first identified the primary user groups: young patients, their adult parents/caregivers, and the hospital's new staff. They then identified the key challenges facing each group and discovered that high stress levels, emotional distress, and a sense of urgency were the top concerns, along with the age of young patients and visitors. The result is a clear information system that reduces stress and environmental graphics that add a sense of joy and vibrancy to the hospital. The team of Dotdash and Conrad Gargett Lyons Architects envisioned a "living tree", with a network of double-height spaces "branches" radiating from two vertical, light-filled atria "trunks". The branch spaces extend to form framing portals for views of key landmarks, including nearby parks, distant mountains, and the Brisbane River.

← Atrium
↙ Exterior wayfinding

↑ Lift directory

The same windows allow views into the building, helping to demystify the hospital experience, particularly for children. Areas of high-contrast color on walls and floors highlight key decision points such as elevator lobbies and entrances, and levels are identified with a palette of bold colors. Dotdash augmented the architectural cues with a system of more than 1,500 wayfinding signs, from super-scaled, 3,800 millimeter sculptural floor identifiers to interior and exterior directionals for the hospital, parking garages, clinical areas, in-patient and outpatient wards, and back of house areas. The scope also included 3,500 room signs.
Another major challenge in the project was how to provide wayfinding assistance to vision-impaired visitors within such a complex building. The solution was to install Braille and tactile signs and TGSIs at key arrival point intercoms where vision-impaired visitors can access wayfinding assistance in a dignified manner.

↑ Emergency entrance

← Lift floor identification green

↓ Map information design

→ Lift foor identification pink
↓ Hospital atrium entrance

designers index

22quadrat www.22quadrat.com 80-83

6D-K www.6d-k.com 122-123, 178-179

Alexander Owen Architecture
www.aoarchitecture.co.uk 10-13, 128-131

ArtHouse Design www.arthousedenver.com 172-175

Benedek & Co. Brand & Design
www.benedek.company 52-53

Blitz www.studioblitz.com 150-151

buero bauer Gesellschaft für Orientierung und Identität
www.buerobauer.com 132-133, 182-183

büro uebele visuelle kommunikation
www.uebele.com 114-117, 162-165

C&G Partners www.cgpartnersllc.com 156-157

Crossboundaries www.crossboundaries.com 158-161

designgruppe koop
www.designgruppe-koop.de 118-121

Dotdash dotdash.com.au 186-189

Endpoint www.weareendpoint.com 26-29, 54-57

Entro www.entro.com 18-21

Form & Fokus
www.form-fokus.de 90-93, 138-141

Benedikt Haid www.benedikt-haid.eu 98-101

Renda Helin Design & Interiors
www.rendahelin.com 104-107

IFUB* GmbH www.ifub.de 142-145

inkl. Design www.inkl.design.de 68-71

Kolektyf www.kolektyf.com 40-43, 166-169

Kuhl|Frenzel www.kuhlfrenzel.de 86-89

La Letterie www.laletterie.com 112-113

Moniteurs GmbH Kommunikationsdesign
www.moniteurs.de 36-39, 134-137

Moscow Design Studio / Polina Chemeris
www.polinachemeris.com 14-17

P-06 Atelier www.p-06-atelier.pt 84-85, 180-181

Pentagram www.pentagram.com 54-57, 176-177

polyform - planen und gestalten
www.polyform-net.de 44-47

Sägenvier DesignKommunikation
www.saegenvier.at 48-51

SKOLNICK Architecture + Design Partnership
www.skolnick.com 64-67

SLANG - Studio for graphic design
www.slanginternational.org 108-111

Studio Eva Plass www.evaplass.de 98-101

studio kw. kommunikationsdesign
www.studiokw.de 124-127

studio polylog www.studio-polylog.com 22-25

Studio Semaphore www.studiosemaphore.com.au 72-75

Studio SÜD–Visuelle Kommunikation
www.studiosued.de 146-149

Studiostaak www.studiostaak.nl 76-79

Sunder-Plassmann & Werner
www.sunder-plassmann-werner.com 58-61

TERADADESIGN ARCHITECTS
www.teradadesign.com 30-31, 184-185

unit-design www.unit-design.de 152-155

Wayfinding Consultores
www.wayfinding.cl 32-35, 94-97

picture credits

22quadrat www.22quadrat.com 80-83
Aldo Amoretti www.aldoamoretti.com 48, 50 a. l.
Daniella Baptista www.daniellabaptista.com 26-29
Filip Basara 40-43
Blinque imagineering 77, 78 b.
Polina Chemeris www.polinachemeris.com 14-17
Chuck Choi www.chuckchoi.com 156
Crossboundaries
www.crossboundaries.com 158 a. r.,159 a.
designgruppe koop
www.designgruppe-koop.de 118-121
Form & Fokus
www.form-fokus.de 90-93, 138-141
Shingo Fujimoto 122-123
Camila González 32, 34 b., 94, 96 a.
Brigida González
www.brigidagonzalez.de 114, 115 b., 116-117, 162-165
Axel Hartmann www.ah-fotografie.de 86-89
Anja Heidenreich 60
HG Esch www.hgesch.de 115 a.
inkl. Design www.inkl.design.de 68-71
Christopher Frederick Jones
www.cfjphoto.com.au 186, 187 a., 188 b. r.
Tsutomu Kawashima 170-171, 178-179
Simon Kennedy
www.simonkennedy.net 54, 55 b., 56, 57 a.
Stephan Klonk
www.klonkfotodesign.de 44 b., 45-47
Karolina Kosowicz 166-169
Haydar Koyupinar 58, 59 a., 61
Max Kropitz www.maxkropitz.com 132-133, 182-183
La Letterie www.laletterie.com 112-113
Felix Löcher www.sichtkreis.com 44 a.
Nico Marques www.nicomarques.com 150-151
Fraser Marsden 72-75
MASI www.enricamasi.me 76, 78 a., 79
Norbert Miguletz 152-155
Florent Moglia 108-111
Yuki Omori 30-31, 184-185
Pentagram www.pentagram.com 55 a., 55 m., 57 b.
Eduardo Perez
www.eduardoperez.de 102-103, 142-145
Eva Plass www.evaplass.de 98-101
Gerald Querubin 18-21
Stefan Schilling
www.stefan-schilling.de 8-9, 36-39, 134-137
Jackie Schumaker
www.jackieshumaker.com 172-175
James Shanks www.jamesshanks.com 176-177
Dianna Snape
www.diannasnape.com 187 b., 188 a., 188 b. l., 189
Tom St. Aubyn www.tomstaubyn.com 10-13, 128-131
Pamela Sthandier 33, 34 a., 35, 95, 96 b., 97
Studio SÜD www.studiosued.de 146-149
David Sundberg www.esto.com 157
Sunder-Plassmann & Werner
www.sunder-plassmann-werner.com 59 b.
Darko Todorovic
www.darkotodorovic.com 49, 50 a. r., 50 b. l., 50 b. r., 51
Chris van Uffelen 6-7
Furkan Uyan www.furkanuyan.com 104-107
José Vicente, Agência Calipo
www.agenciacalipo.com 62-63, 84-85, 180-181
Bernd Vogel, studio polylog
www.studio-polylog.com 22-25
Louis Volkmann www.louisvolkmann.net 124-127
Jonathan Wallen www.jonathanwallen.com 64-65
Ola Wilk / Wilk Marketing Communications 66-67
Xia Zhi www.xiazhipictures.com 158 a. l. a., 158 a. l. b., 159 b., 161

Cover front: Benedek & Co. Brand & Design
Cover back (from left to right, from above to below): James Shanks; Ola Wilk / Wilk Marketing Communications; Norbert Miguletz; José Vicente, Agência Calipo

imprint

The Deutsche Nationalbibliothek lists this publication in the Deutsche Nationalbibliografie; detailed bibliographic data are available on the Internet at http://dnb.dnb.de

ISBN 978-3-03768-239-5

www.braun-publishing.ch

1st edition 2021

Editor Redaktionsbüro van Uffelen / Editorial office
Editorial staff and layout
Andrea Büchel, Michael Bungardt, Julia Habenicht
Graphic concept Benjamin Wolbergs
Reproduction Bild1Druck, Berlin